The Farmer as Manager

The Farmer as Manager

SECOND EDITION

by

Tony Giles

*Professor of Farm Management and
Director of the Farm Management Unit
University of Reading*

&

Malcolm Stansfield

*Senior Lecturer and
Deputy Director of the Farm Management Unit
University of Reading*

C·A·B International

C·A·B International
Wallingford
Oxon OX10 8DE
UK

Tel: Wallingford (0491) 32111
Telex: 847964 (COMAGG G)
Telecom Gold/Dialcom: 84: CAU001
Fax: (0491) 33508

British Library Cataloguing in Publication Data
Giles, A. K. (Anthony Kent) *1928–*
    The farmer as manager.–2nd ed.
    1. Great Britain. Agricultural industries. Farms.
Management
    I. Title   II. Stansfield, Malcolm
    630.68

    ISBN 0-85198-673-0

Printed and bound in Great Britain by Bookcraft (Bath) Ltd

Contents

Preface to the Second Edition   vii
Acknowledgements   viii

Part I Introducing Management

1 About this Book   3
2 About Management   6

Part II Managers' Functions

3 Setting Objectives   19
4 Planning   31
5 Decision-Making   44
6 Control   58

Part III What has to be Managed?

7 Production   75
8 Buying and Selling   102
9 Finance   117
10 Staff   155

Part IV The Manager

11 Managing the Manager   173
12 Acquiring Information   183
13 Priorities   193
14 Summary, Afterthoughts and Conclusions   198

Postscript   205
Index   206

Preface to the Second Edition

This book was originally dedicated 'to all those who at one time or another have helped us to develop our views and who (originally) encouraged us to write them down'.

The fact that many of the principles originally discussed have not seriously altered suggests that we were helped to get them more or less right in the first place. The context in which they are applied, however, is changing constantly and, as we hope our revised text reflects, has changed very substantially during the decade which has separated the first edition of this book from the second.

Acknowledgements

ON THE FIRST EDITION

The authors are especially grateful to Harold Casey, Richard Clarke, Graham Dalton, Michael Dart, Edgar Thomas, Don Salmon and Stuart Wragg, all of whom, in their different capacities, have given helpful comments on either the layout or the contents of this book – without trying to persuade us to write something substantially different from our original intentions.

We would also like to thank Mrs Audrey Collins, Miss Sue Pipe and Miss Carol Rees who, between them, have typed and retyped the manuscript; our families who, while it was being written, forfeited a summer holiday, with hardly a murmur; and, finally, John Churchill and Roger Jones, of George Allen & Unwin, who guided us patiently through the inevitable hiccups.

ON THE SECOND EDITION

We remain grateful to all those mentioned above and more recently to Tim Hardwick and his colleagues of C·A·B International for their confidence in backing this revised edition; to Roger Jones, Clem Earle and their colleagues at Unwin Hyman for relinquishing their publishing rights; to colleagues (especially Giles Martin) who prepare annually our departmental publication *Farm Business Data*, from which we have drawn material; and to Mrs Sheila Smith and Mrs Maxine Oakes who have typed our fresh manuscript.

Tony Giles
Malcolm Stansfield

PART I

Introducing Management

Chapter 1

About this Book

I purposefully avoid cramming the book with
facts, figures and details. It is a book about...
plans and the ways... to carry them through.
Mikhail Gorbachev
Perestroika, 1987

We, also, have purposely avoided cramming this book with facts, figures and details. It is a book that we hope will be read, digested and reflected on, rather than used as a manual. We have tried to offer directions and ideas, but decisions are left to the reader, and the full details of particular techniques that he or she may wish to use in reaching those decisions are more likely to be found in other books.

Indeed, it should be emphasized at the outset that this book is about farming only in the sense that it is about the management of farms, and frequently it will be argued by us – while acknowledging that every industry has its own special technical problems, and farming may feel it has more than its share of them – that management is management wherever it is practised. Here we are concerned with the practice of managing farms.

This book is directed primarily towards farmers and salaried farm managers; however, since we have concerned ourselves with the responsibilities and problems which confront all those who manage farms in whatever capacity, we hope that what we have written will also be of value to other groups of readers: primarily, to those who teach, research into, or advise on farm management; secondly, to those in other professions who have to deal with, and therefore understand, farmers; and thirdly, to students who in the short term have to pass examinations in farm management, and who may eventually either be managing farms themselves, or be in one of the other related occupations referred to above.

With these various readers in mind – but especially those who are already managing or are about to manage farms – the book is divided into four parts. There are two introductory chapters – this one introducing the book itself and the second introducing management as a discipline. There are then four chapters which deal in turn with certain basic functions for which managers have to be responsible: setting objectives, planning, decision-making and control. These chapters are followed by four which discuss the principal areas over which management has to operate in any business: production, marketing, finance and staffing. Before the concluding chapter, there are three which concentrate on the managers themselves: on how they organize themselves, acquire information and set priorities.

Each chapter is preceded by a short summary to aid the reader. Then at the end of each chapter (apart from the first and the last ones) the reader will find three things:

- Our final thoughts
- Questions and exercises
- A guide to further reading.

Our 'final thoughts' are simply the thoughts with which we would like to leave the reader. They reflect something of the shared philosophy that the authors have on many (but not all!) aspects of management. Perhaps, therefore, they are our first thoughts as well as our last.

The questions are not intended to be an examination for the reader but rather to provide a check on the extent to which the principal message contained in each chapter has been understood and remembered. Occasional reference back to them might be a convenient way of recalling material that has been read. They may also provide the basis for discussion at farmers' meetings and other occasions.

The annotated references to other works are mainly offered where the further elaboration of an idea or technique would have been beyond the intended scope and length of this book, or because we would like to encourage further reading in certain areas. These references have been carefully selected and have been very strictly limited in number; we know that we are addressing busy people.

This short introductory chapter would not be complete without some brief reference to what the reader might hope to find but will not. The point has already been made that this book is about management, not about husbandry as such, although husbandry skills are, of course, an integral part of the overall business of managing a farm and will be referred to as examples of specific managerial functions such as setting objectives, planning, decision-making and control, which are all relevant to farming. Neither is the book about agricultural economics in the broad sense, nor about very esoteric planning and appraisal techniques which are unlikely to feature strongly, if at all, in most farmers' managerial toolbags. We are not suggesting that such techniques have no place in farming; we know, of course, that they have, but when they are needed, farmers may often rely on the expertise of appropriately trained advisers and consultants. We will indicate where and when such techniques may be useful, and where they are fully described in contemporary farm management literature. In discussing and using techniques, however, we have deliberately refrained from attaching too many monetary figures to our examples, for two reasons. First, we would be bound to use £'s which is offputting to readers outside the UK – of whom we know there have been many. But, secondly, even when rounded off, figures at once become out of date, giving an ephemeral nature to the text which we hope it is not.

Finally, there are a number of topics which are either highly specialized or peculiar to the UK and to this point in time. Numerous aspects of legal and fiscal arrangements (e.g. company law, taxation) fall squarely into this category as do many instruments of government policy. Although we are mindful of the way in which these and many other aspects of the wider social environment impinge upon the individual farmer and farm manager, we have excluded any detailed considerations of them for two reasons. Firstly, although working and writing in the UK – and inevitably using mainly domestic examples to illustrate our text – we have aimed (in both the first edition, and here) to provide a book that will interest an international farming readership, and that will not quickly become outdated. Secondly, we recognize that there is a range of 'internal' influences, of the kind referred to, which need to be written about by specialists in specific books. Neither of us feels qualified to claim to be such a specialist.

There is one more thing to mention here. It would be tedious to refer throughout the book to 'farmers and farm managers' when we simply mean 'those who manage farms'. The two groups are, of course, in different situations – one, self-employed with capital at risk, the other, salaried with a job at risk. In many respects, however – and certainly on a day-to-day basis – they do the same job, that is, manage farm businesses. So unless otherwise stated, when we refer either to farmers or farm managers, we have both groups in mind.

Chapter 2

About Management

Defining management
Clothing the definition
The external environment
Management applied to farms
Farm management and general management literature

DEFINING MANAGEMENT

A definition is not a bad point from which to start discussing any subject. But it is not always easy – especially with such a complex subject as management.

There are probably as many different definitions of management as there are authors who have written about it and managers who practise it. These differences arise for a variety of reasons: sometimes from profitless debate about whether management is an art or a science; sometimes reflecting the different standpoints from which individuals approach the subject; and sometimes from the different purposes for which the definition is required. The usual pattern is for definitions to fall into one of two main categories: either the short, sharp ones that try to say it all in a pithy sentence or two; or those that, in the interest of omitting nothing of importance, become a tortuously long discourse rather than a definition – and so defeat the object of the exercise.

The authors favour the first category, and the simple statement:

management is about deciding what you want to do, and then doing it

This definition puts the emphasis on two key aspects of management – making decisions and implementing them – and yet it says nothing at all about what those two activities entail, and may be in danger of implying that management is simple: first decide what you have to do and then get on and do it!

Nothing, of course, could be further from the truth than the idea that management is ever simple, and it is perhaps significant that the doyen of management gurus, Peter Drucker, seldom offers any short and neat definitions of management. In one of his recent articles*, for instance, he answers the question 'What is management?' with seven separate statements, each of which he elaborates, and only the core of which is reproduced here. 'Management', he says:

- is about human beings;
- is deeply embedded in culture;
- requires simple, clear and unifying objectives;
- should enable the enterprise and its members to grow and develop;
- is built on communications and individual responsibility;
- must be judged by a variety of measures ... not by the bottom line alone;
- has no results inside its walls; results exist only on the outside – with a satisfied customer.

We would like to think that each of these precepts is embraced in this book. We choose, however, to start with our own definition of management which is deliberately void of any agricultural connotations and is as follows:

Management is a comprehensive activity, involving the combination and co-ordination of human, physical and financial resources, in a way which produces a commodity or a service which is both wanted and can be offered at a price which will be paid, while making the working environment for those involved agreeable and acceptable.

This is the definition that we offered in the first edition of this book and we have decided, ten years on, not to change it. We are aware, of course, that there are many non-commercial activities and organizations that have to be managed, but are not necessarily concerned with *selling* a product or service and for whom, therefore, 'a price which will be paid' may not be a key issue. Even in these cases, however, resources are still being used and it is unlikely that, in some sense, the books do not eventually have to be balanced. For this reason, and because we are concerned in this book with managing a business situation – albeit of a particular kind – we have decided to stick with the market flavour of our definition; with Drucker's 'satisfied customers'.

We hope that we have not fallen into the trap of turning our definition into a discourse. It has, however, been deliberately worded so as to draw

---

*Drucker, P. F. (1988) Management and the World's Work. *Harvard Business Review*, September/October.

attention to a number of aspects of management which we believe to be of central importance and which a shorter definition could not encompass.

First, it shows that management does not have narrow boundaries. The delegation of various aspects of management may or may not be possible, depending upon the size of an organization. In most small businesses (which is what the majority of farms are) the opportunities for the delegation of management are strictly limited. But delegation or not, top management ultimately has the responsibility for all that goes on. Management can never, therefore, be less than a comprehensive process.

Secondly, management is concerned with combination: with the combination of a number of different and separate factors of production – land, labour and capital – into an effective and viable production unit. The classical economic questions about production – what to produce, in what combination and by what methods – are at the heart of this aspect of the manager's task.

Thirdly, our definition points to the need for managers to be market-orientated. Attention needs to be kept carefully fixed on an end product: the product (or service) must be wanted by consumers and it must be supplied at a price they are willing to pay. The mind is thus immediately focused not just on production, but on effective production in economic terms, and that means the long-term survival of the business on a sound financial basis.

And finally, there is emphasis on the human factor. We believe that in any business situation the provision of agreeable and acceptable working conditions may be as important an element in the long-term survival of that business as is profit itself. The importance of this most influential and variable of all resources cannot be overemphasized and we make no apology, therefore, for the final clause of our definition.

CLOTHING THE DEFINITION

If a definition is a necessary starting point, it is just as necessary to move beyond it and to develop and clothe the initial statement. It is all very well to use academic-sounding phrases like 'the co-ordination of human, physical and financial resources', but what does it mean, or more important still, what should it mean, in terms of actually managing an organization? What picture of management as a practical task emerges from the clothing of our definition?

Attempts to describe the work of managers tend to fall into one of two categories: the prescriptive and the descriptive. The first concentrates on what managers ought to do, and the second on what they actually do. This book probably falls somewhere between the two approaches with some combination of principles and practice. This particular chapter, however, is more concerned with principles. When we move beyond our definition the framework of management which emerges in our minds is the one shown in Fig. 2.1.

Without becoming unhelpfully complicated, no diagram of this kind can hope to be comprehensive, nor should it be regarded as sacrosanct. It will always depict a personal view of how the manager's task can be envisaged and thought about. Such a diagram will do a disservice if it is thought to reflect the whole story, or if it suggests that the main processes depicted (setting objectives, planning, decision-making and controlling) or the main *sectors* of the business (production, marketing, financing and staffing) are separate and independent of each other. All of those involved in farm management will know that this is not the case. Such a diagram does, however, have the merit of identifying the key areas of responsibility and activity, and serves the purpose of keeping each of these responsibilities and activities in perspective, and of demonstrating the extent of the manager's task.

Our particular diagram has been constructed in order to carry a few

Fig. 2.1. The framework of management.

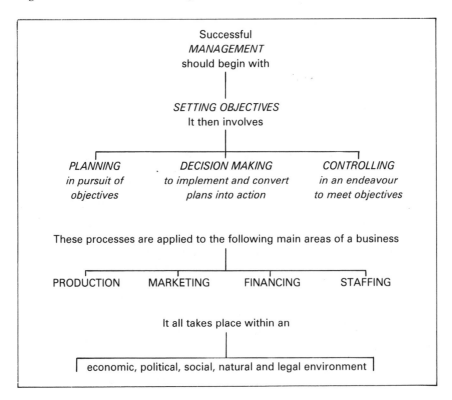

clear messages to the reader about our view of management; in particular, perhaps, that to be effective (and who is interested in ineffective management?) management should begin with a careful consideration of objectives. That word does not appear in our definition. It is, however, the thread which runs through it and without which no clear directions can be followed and no meaningful assessment can be made of subsequent achievement. The setting of objectives, in fact, is the point from which we begin our detailed examination of management and is considered in detail in Chapter 3. Assuming, however, that it is possible to identify and quantify certain objectives, then clear courses of action are necessary if those objectives are to be achieved. First, plans must be devised in each relevant area of the organization or business which permit the stated objectives to be pursued. Those plans will need to be constantly updated with changing economic and other circumstances, and must then be put into operation, or kept in operation, as a result of decisions that managers must take. Indeed, some writers on management have been inclined to equate the central task of management with the decision-making process – a view that we shall consider later. Setting objectives, devising plans and making decisions will be a waste of effort unless care is taken to ensure that what is required to happen does actually happen. If it does not, then the reasons for this need to be known and understood, and, wherever possible, corrective action needs to be taken. In other words, control must be exercised.

To a large extent it is the responsibility for these matters – setting objectives, planning, decision-making and controlling – which characterizes the manager's role. He or she will be required to exercise these responsibilities in respect of each staff section or area of his business, which means, as we have indicated, production, marketing, financing and staffing. If the manager is not the owner of the business, he or she undertakes the stewardship of the business on behalf of its owners. But if he or she is the owner, then the manager will accept the final risk for the capital that is at stake.

It is appreciated that this brief view of the manager's task may represent more or less than the whole story for many businesses and indeed for some farms. On the small one-man farm, for instance, with perhaps no labour other than that provided by the farmer himself, there will be no staffing problems as such, although there will still be problems of labour organization. Increasingly on farms there may be a conservation activity which has to be managed but does not really fall into any of the four business sections mentioned. Similarly, on some farms (for example, those run by educational establishments) there may be a research and development section quite separate from routine commercial production. For many situations, however, it is believed that this fourfold division is appropriate.

It is also appreciated that there is a close interaction between each of these sections. Decisions about what, when and how to produce have immediate and obvious repercussions on marketing arrangements, on capital requirements and on the number and quality of staff to be employed. In a similar way, decisions which relate primarily to questions of capital supply or to the availability of labour will have an important influence on production possibilities. Examples of such interactions are endless, particularly in respect to changes in production patterns, often in response to external influences, which can have a ripple effect throughout the business.

THE EXTERNAL ENVIRONMENT

No business, and therefore no farm, exists or operates in a vacuum. Constraints of various kinds – social, legal, natural, political and economic, sometimes emanating from forces (especially economic forces) well beyond national boundaries – constantly affect the freedom of managers. Increasingly it becomes the task of managers to try to understand and adapt to these changing forces. A detailed analysis of these forces is well beyond the scope of this book, but has recently been explored elsewhere by the authors in the review of the Manager's Environment referred to at the end of this chapter. Matters such as the way in which prices and costs are influenced by international markets, the prevailing climate for borrowing funds, the effect of legal constraints in the field of employment, social responsibilities in respect of such questions as pollution and other environmental issues, as well as the influence of purely political considerations on national farming policies and international agreements, are just some of the more obvious examples of the various influences which combine to create the environment in which managers have to work. As we enter the last decade of this century major developments such as the completion of the single market in Europe, increased international pressures through GATT negotiations to decrease world-wide agricultural protection, and the growing public concern over a wide range of food safety and 'green' issues (including the gradual approach of the greenhouse effect) will, we believe, increase rather than decrease the external constraining influences on farmers. Such influences of various kinds affect the whole business community in one way or another. Few managers will need reminding that these influences are real, usually unavoidable and just have to be lived with. At the end of the day, farm managers, like all other managers, must simply get on and manage.

MANAGEMENT APPLIED TO FARMS

The purpose of this chapter has been to discuss the nature of management in a general way, although as it has progressed it has been natural for us to begin to introduce a farming flavour both in terms of the particular problems and interactions that exist for farmers within their businesses (the internal environment) and the external influences which constrain them – and, of course, create their opportunities (the external environment). We do not believe, however, that their particular managerial problems should distance farm managers from other managers in the economy quite as much as sometimes seems to have been the case. All managers have much in common in terms of the functions they perform and the main segments of their businesses that have to be managed. They all have their own particular internal and external problems, and if farming can identify itself more closely with the rest of the business world – as we believe it is doing – this will be to its long-term advantage. We have sometimes suggested that it may even be debatable whether it is helpful to think about 'farm management' as a subject in its own right at all. It may be more rewarding to think simply in terms of management applied to farms, with the technical problems of farming falling into their appropriate place alongside all the others; hence the title of this book.

One of the classic books to be written on this subject in the post-war era was Dexter and Barber's *Farming For Profits*, first published in 1960 by Penguin. Much of it is now well out of date but the philosophical approach of the early chapters remains excellent reading. They had none of our qualms about referring to farm management as a subject which, they wrote:

> is concerned with the organisation and deployment of the resources put into a farm business – the land, the capital, the labour and that item of over-riding importance, the ability and skills of the individual farmer. It is not, in our opinion, concerned with the purely technical matters in farming, nor, on the other hand, is it concerned with the best way of giving the orders to the staff at seven o'clock in the morning. These questions do arise but they are subordinate to the main consideration of organising a farm for higher profit.
>
> (Dexter and Barber, 1960, pp. 13–14)

We would not argue with this description; and (despite the reference here to high profit as the main consideration) neither would we disagree with Drucker that management should not be judged by the bottom line alone. Our position about profits is clear. They permit and encourage survival – which must be the ultimate long-term aim of all management. Profits are not the only thing that matters, but, without them, bankruptcy may follow by which time it is too late for anything else to matter. It is also our belief that farms are likely to be successfully managed, and profits generated, if certain general principles of management are understood and applied to farm businesses, just as they should be to other businesses and organizations. This is not to say that we wish to belittle the importance of good husbandry and of doing things well technically. On the contrary, it is very important to do things well, and it will seldom, in fact, be in conflict with doing things profitably. It is common knowledge that it is the last few eggs, piglets, litres of milk or kilos of corn which produce the profit. We will return to this subject in Chapter 7, which deals with production, but at this stage we wish to emphasize (as Dexter and Barber did) our belief that too much preoccupation with the purely technical and with day-to-day matters could be dangerous if it is at the expense of the more strategic, commercial and human aspects of management. To be caught in the so-called 'activity trap' – too busy with the immediate to think about the important – could spell the opposite of survival.

FARM MANAGEMENT AND GENERAL MANAGEMENT LITERATURE

There is one last point that we wish to make in this chapter. It concerns reading. We have already, in Chapter 1, made it clear that it is not the purpose of this book to go into great detail about particular farm manage-ment business techniques. To do so would not have produced the kind of book that we wished to write and would have merely duplicated what is available in other books. There are several in the UK to which the reader can turn: Barnard and Nix; Norman, Turner and Wilson; Warren; Buckett; and Turner and Taylor. Each of these books is valuable in its particular way and each has its strong area of detail. Similar texts exist in other coun-tries, one of the best examples being from the USA, Boehlje and Eidman's *Farm Management.* The full reference to all of these books is given at the end of this chapter and they will be referred to more selectively throughout the book. The reader is also advised to make use of the Centre of Manage-ment in Agriculture's excellent journal *Farm Management.* It provides a valuable means of remaining up to date, and a recent published subject index assists the easy recall of what has appeared in the Journal over more than 20 years – much of which does not easily date.

All of the references will have their use in a strictly 'farm management' context. If as we have suggested, however, management is management wherever it is applied, those concerned with the management of farms should not ignore the general management literature. There is a vast array of information not all of an equal standard. Drucker has already been mentioned; always readable, always thought-provoking. Any one of his books is worth reading and would lead to others. *The Effective Executive* remains, despite its vintage, a firm favourite with us, but more recently, *The Changing World of the Executive* covers Drucker's usual wide range. Other, more biographical, management books include American busi-nessman Victor Kiam's *Going For It* and, in the UK, the retired John Harvey-Jones' *Making It Happen.* More academic is Peters and

Waterman's popular *In Search of Excellence.*

We cannot stress too strongly to our readers that they should augment any strictly farm management reading with this wider management reading. The former is most likely to help in the application of particular techniques and the solution of particular problems. The latter is more likely to stimulate thought across a wider range of management issues and to assist in meeting the challenges of the times.

OUR FINAL THOUGHT

It may be more helpful to think in terms of management applied to farms than of farm management as a subject in its own right; farmers and farm managers should avoid thinking of themselves as managerially unique.

QUESTIONS AND EXERCISES

- Write your own definition of management. Then compare it with the one by Drucker summarized in this chapter, and consider any differences.

- Look critically at our diagrammatic representation of management and then draw your own.

- What aspects of management do you find most difficult? List them; then write down why you find them difficult and what you can do about each difficulty.

- Select one general management book from the list below, that you haven't read – then buy it and read it.

GUIDE TO FURTHER READING

Some stimulating general books on management

In our view, an excursion into a few of these books is essential for the manager who wants his or her business to survive.

Blanchard, K. and Johnson, S. (1983) *The One Minute Manager.* Mellow Books, London.
    A cult book – a brief but inspiring read.

Drucker, P. F. (1982) *The Changing World of the Executive.* Heinemann, London.

A collection of essays covering a wide range of topics. Not intended to be read from cover to cover but for dipping into. We also recommend any of Drucker's other books, especially some of his earlier general work, such as *The Practice of Management, The Effective Executive, Managing for Results* and *Management,* all available in Pan Books.

Harvey-Jones, J. (1988) *Making It Happen.* Collins, London.
A pleasure to read. Autobiographical reflections on leadership and many other aspects of management.

Kiam, V. (1986) *Going For It!* Collins, London.
A very readable autobiographical challenge to your entrepreneurship.

Peters, T. J. and Waterman, R. H. (1982) *In Search of Excellence.* Harper and Row, London.
Your management reading is not complete without this book.

The standard (UK) texts on farm management

Each of these books has its strengths and weaknesses and is written at the particular level to which it is addressed.

Barnard, C. S. and Nix, J. S. (1979) *Farm Planning and Control,* 2nd edn. Cambridge University Press, Cambridge.
The 'heavyweight' – indispensable for those reading to degree level.

Boehlje, M. D. and Eidman, V. R. (1984) *Farm Management.* Wiley, New York.
The US counterpart of Barnard and Nix.

Buckett, M. (1988) *An Introduction to Farm Organisation and Management,* 2nd edn. Pergamon, Oxford.
Written primarily for the post-certificate and diploma levels, it is somewhat uneven in its treatment, but scores in places with impressive treatment of details often glossed over by other authors.

Norman, L., Turner R. and Wilson, K. (1985) *The Farm Business,* 2nd edn. Longman, London.
Written originally with City and Guilds examinations in mind this book could help readers at all levels. Strong on practical examples and the management of individual enterprises.

Turner, J. and Taylor, M. (1989) *Applied Farm Management.* BSP Professional Books, Oxford.
Covers, in varying depths, the whole of the conventional farm management field, but is strongest on areas that most other farm management books skirt round, such as marketing and policy.

Warren, F. M. (1986) *Financial Management for Farmers,* 2nd edn. Hutchinson, London.
Goes beyond the purely financial, but is strong on that field, with extensive worked examples. Particularly valuable for those who need to overcome the financial bogey.

See also the 'Management/Managers' heading of the 'Subject Index of Articles Appearing in the First Six Volumes of *Farm Management*' (CMA Journal) in **Vol. 7 No. 1.**, Spring 1989.

PART II

Managers' Functions

Chapter 3

Setting Objectives

The need for objectives
Determining objectives
Advantages of the MBO approach
Difficulties of the MBO approach
Summary and limitations

THE NEED FOR OBJECTIVES

Having established what this book is about, we can safely turn our attention to the first, and one of the most important, parts of any manager's job: the setting of objectives. It is increasingly accepted that it is important for any organization to take a periodic look at its broad objectives for a limited number of years ahead, say three to five years. This helps to give the organization itself a purpose, provides the individuals in the organization with a common goal and minimizes the risks of going off at too many tangents.

Objectives in this context are never likely to be in the singular and are seldom likely to be simple. There will always be conflicts and compromises, and profit, important as it will always be, will have to be balanced with other requirements. 'To manage a business', writes Drucker, 'is to balance a variety of needs and goals'.

Farming, like other industries, has its yardsticks by which the financial results for any particular trading year can be assessed and judged. Simple comparisons with previous years' results, with results drawn from groups of other roughly similar farms or even with tailor-made budgets for the particular farm, all have their uses; but they also have their limitations. In this chapter we are concerned with something more fundamental: with what a business has to offer; with its potential; with what the individuals concerned want out of it; and with what path it is going to follow.

Clarity of thought on fundamental issues of this kind will not be achieved quickly or easily, or without some consultation. But it is only really within the context of some broadly agreed and preferably quantified long-term objectives – or 'goals' as they are often called – that shorter term performance has much meaning. It is difficult to talk about effectiveness or the lack of it – about success or failure – without some reference back to the kind of long-term objectives that this chapter is about.

As well as being a very important aspect of management, setting objectives is notoriously difficult. It is difficult because it is elusive and complicated; it is always moving away from you, always involving conflicting strands of thought and frequently defying attempts to be precise. It also requires concentration, and most of us know only too well how difficult that is, especially if (like many farmers) we have become accustomed to constant interruptions and to a fragmentation of the working day. None us needs reminding of how easy it is to put off jobs that we find difficult, particularly if they are not pressing. What we cannot stress too strongly, however, is that although there may be jobs that are queuing up to be attended to, there are unlikely to be jobs that are more important to the long-term survival of a business than thinking seriously about where it is going and how it is going to get there. That, in essence, is what setting objectives is about. It must be done from time to time, despite the many obstacles that may stand in the way; and it would, in our opinion, be unfortunate if farmers and farm managers ever felt that they were faced with more difficulties in this respect than their counterparts in other sectors of the economy.

DETERMINING OBJECTIVES

We can imagine the reader at this stage having no difficulty in agreeing with the need to have objectives. It is so abundantly sensible to think in this way. But, equally, we can imagine him or her pondering hard over how to actually set about the exercise. The difficulties have been referred to. They are real. Most of us really do feel too busy to deal with anything that is not immediately urgent. We are also usually deterred from starting anything that we are not sure how to start, and which could bring with it the personal discomfort of firm commitments in the future.

In recent years **management by objectives** (hereafter referred to as MBO) has gained ground throughout many industries and organizations as perhaps the most comprehensive and helpful approach to this apparently daunting task. We have already said that this book will not concern itself in detail with techniques – but in this case we make no apology for saying a little about the subject. After all, it is specifically and justifiably claimed for

MBO that it is not really a technique; that it is a way of thinking about the whole management process and about a whole business or organization. That makes it entirely relevant to the thinking that underlies this chapter.

We do not wish to preach a textbook approach to the application of MBO, which we believe would be inappropriate to the fairly informal way in which small businesses are usually managed. We believe, however, that the essence of the approach is entirely appropriate to many, if not all, farm situations and includes the following steps.

1. Discussions, over a period of time, by an appropriately chosen small group of people concerned with the management of a business including, often, somebody from outside the business itself, e.g. an adviser and/or banker;
2. Full discussions of the external environment in which the business is operating and the opportunities that are available to it, to keep the business one jump ahead of events;
3. Careful analysis of the resources which are already available, or which could be introduced, to the business and the possibilities and constraints that, therefore, present themselves. Increasingly these will include issues other than the more traditional technical and economic ones;
4. Clear statements, acceptable to all concerned, about where in the longer term the business is aiming to be, and how in the shorter term it plans to get there;
5. An acceptance by all concerned of the performance levels that are assumed in the plans, and a commitment to achieve them;
6. The quantification of as much of the plans as possible;
7. A recognition of the key results areas of the business, in which it is very important to get good results, either narrowly, in terms of performance within a particular unit or section of a business, or more broadly, in areas of strategic importance, e.g. marketing, employee–employer relations;
8. The setting up of an adequate control system to monitor, correct and adjust plans and objectives;
9. A willingness, periodically, to reconsider, re-plan, re-state and re-dedicate.

There is much more to MBO than this, but we believe that in the context of farming and managers of farms, these points embrace its essential philosophy. Many successful farmers would no doubt claim that they have always done these things and thought in this way, but less formally and without calling it MBO. We have no doubt, from our experience, that they are right. But equally we have no doubt that the formality of MBO as outlined here, applied periodically to the whole business, does have something extra to offer even to the most progressive farmers and farm managers, and that there are many others for whom this approach would offer an almost totally new and beneficial dimension to their management skills and aspirations.

We would not wish to be accused of over-enthusing in this matter. Indeed it is important, in the management world, that new techniques or approaches to problems are seen for what they are and are neither hailed as panaceas nor rejected out of hand as the latest gimmick. MBO is, of course, no longer new, and it would be an exaggeration to pretend that it has had anything resembling widespread application in the farming industry. We believe that this is a pity, and that, as new ideas emerge from the world and literature of management, MBO should not be gradually lost sight of as another gimmick that came and went. We would like to see more serious examples of its application than we know of, in a style that is both relevant and acceptable to the farming industry.

The right approach, for instance, might call for a farmhouse meeting on rather a formal basis with objective setting as the sole item on the agenda. This does not mean that it will all be over quickly! The form of the meeting and numbers attending will vary considerably according to the size and complexity of the business. With the small family unit, discussions may involve only the farmer and his wife, or her husband, but more usually, and especially in larger businesses, the directors would ideally be joined by senior managers as well as consultants. In a family business where two or three generations are actively involved, the chairman might well have an important role to fulfil. More than one session will almost certainly be required in order to agree a series of goals – but the outcome should be a list, quantified whenever possible, of what is to be achieved, how and when.

THE ADVANTAGES OF THE MBO APPROACH

Approached in this way we can see several important benefits that the underlying philosophy of MBO, however informally applied, can offer the farming industry in particular. There are four benefits that we would like to mention.

First, there is the importance of confronting oneself with what may be called 'square one' questions. To those who are not steeped in the jargon and style of modern business management techniques, the answers to questions like 'What business are we in?' or 'Who are our customers?' might seem so obvious, or so irrelevant to getting on with the job in hand, as to be a waste of time. And yet these are precisely the kinds of questions which may help to clarify thinking, eliminate the unimportant and impractical, and concentrate thinking on those areas of activity on which success is most likely to depend, i.e. on the key results areas. If the value of trying to answer basic questions of this kind is in doubt it is worth noting that Robert

Townsend (in *Up The Organisation*) describes how this company took six months to agree on a simple 23-word objective that, he says, 'was simple enough that we didn't have to write it down ... (but) ... it included a definition of our business ... (and) ... let us put the blinders on ourselves'. Don't be frightened, therefore, especially in these days of 'diversification', to spend time reflecting on such basic questions as what business are you in, who your customers are, what scale and kind of operation you envisage managing, and what kind of returns you seek. As the direct interface between the farming community and individual members of the public grows, clear notions of just where farming begins and ends are becoming less and less easy to identify. The provision of such services as bed and breakfast, retail milk-rounds and nature trails create a wide range of possible answers to the questions posed above. But everything else will build on the answers to those questions. It will be a salutary exercise and you are unlikely to progress far with it on your own.

Secondly, there is the advantage of a periodic and thorough consideration of the resources at your disposal. Again this may seem so obvious as not to require any special attention. But a thorough appraisal and understanding of the variability and the flexibility of the resources at your command – those that you own and those that you might borrow, share or hire – will be at the heart of all forward planning. Constraints on the opportunities that you can grasp will be provided more by those resources than by anything else. Land, labour and capital are all available to you in limited amounts and each will usually be far from homogenous in character. The variability and potential, for instance, of different soil types within the farm boundary and the extent to which that potential can be influenced by the application of technology; the skill and experience of your staff; the quality and flexibility of fixed capital equipment, and the availability of liquid (or near liquid) capital: all of these things will have an important influence on what is possible and what is not. Their potential and their alternative uses should not be taken for granted. Nor should the potential for strengthening and developing the use of existing and new resources resulting from collaboration between farmers. Group activities can open up new possibilities in numerous areas of farming, with production methods, marketing and training coming instantly to mind. Many British farmers continue to lag behind their international counterparts in this respect but we see it as an aspect of farm business management to which more thought and energy could profitably be devoted.

Thirdly, when carrying out this kind of appraisal it would be wrong for managers to fall into the trap of believing that they, themselves, were not part of the parcel of resources that they manage; and a very important part into the bargain. We will discuss this topic – managing the manager – in a later chapter. It is sufficient at this stage simply to recognize the fact, and the importance of management as an influence on the effectiveness of other staff and general conduct of any business. A serious exercise in self-appraisal is, therefore, a very special part of the wider examination of the resources just discussed. An honest appreciation of one's own personal aims and ambitions, as well as one's talents and limitations, will be important ingredients in setting realistic and obtainable objectives. It will not be easy and, again, it will almost certainly be unachievable without the stimulation of discussion with others.

Finally, we wish to stress the importance of a consideration of the so-called external environment. This is in contrast to the internal environment discussed in the previous paragraph. Equally important, but perhaps more difficult to be at all precise about, it consists of those factors, national and international, that are largely economic, social and political in character, and that provide the environment within which any business must operate. No business operates in isolation. Understanding that environment, in all its complexity, is beyond most of us. But being aware of the more obvious commercial and political forces and trends at work, and being alert to the opportunities and constraints that they may present to your particular business, is essential. It is not an easy job. It calls for an awareness which, fortunately, many farmers seem to possess as an integral part of their character. Selective reading, listening and discussion will all play their part in this process, the accumulated results of which should certainly find their place in any overall review of a firm's objectives. There will be a fuller consideration of the importance of acquiring information in another chapter but it should be stated here that a keen awareness of the fresh opportunities that form an on-going part of the external environment can make the essential difference between a traditional manager who is always one step behind and the genuine entrepreneur who is one step ahead. In a changing and increasingly competitive world, in which the farming community is being invited to rely more and more on market forces, we believe that the application of MBO could encourage the entrepreneurial style on which survival will increasingly depend.

THE DIFFICULTIES OF THE MBO APPROACH

In advocating the approach of management by objectives and drawing attention to some of the advantages that it can offer, we are mindful of the difficulties that are involved and of its limitations. The difficulties are alluded to earlier in the chapter. It is an elusive and complicated exercise, always involving conflicting strands of thought. These conflicts can take several forms.

First, there is the conflict between the short and the long term. These time periods are not easily defined, but the short term is usually a year or two at the most, while the long term is somewhere between five and at the very most ten years. What is certain is that there will sometimes be conflict between a desire to make gradual progress towards long-term objectives and the need to contend with more immediate short-term objectives and problems. The two will often compete both for time and capital and there may be no escape from this situation. It may be an irritation, but it is a situation that must be accepted. Drucker often warns that the nature of a particular business, and of different sectors within a particular business, will have an influence on how far ahead objectives can reasonably be set and on what constitutes the short or the long term. In a farming context, for instance, the gradual building up of a livestock enterprise, and the installation of accompanying buildings and equipment, may be a clear long-term objective. The need, however, to improve the performance within an existing herd or flock at its existing size, or to get more animals quickly in order to improve cash flows and profits, may be a more pressing short-term objective, the achievement of which might easily defer the achievement of the longer term objective. What is important in this kind of situation is the ability of management to identify priorities, a subject we give special space towards the end of the book. Judgement will be required and so will flexibility. It will always be important to look ahead to the technology of five years' time, but without jeopardizing what needs to be done well today. Too much concentration on long-term possibilities – sitting back, for example, waiting for a neighbouring farm to come on the market – at the expense of short-term necessities is a not uncommon reason for disappointing results. A balance, as in most things, is what is required.

A balance is also required in the conflict between a manager's professional and personal lives. The complexity of this kind of conflict is one that few of us escape from, no matter what our job happens to be. It is indeed the acute awareness of such complexities that caused us to choose as the cover for this revised edition of this book not the split-personality (part wellie-booted and part bowler-hatted farmer) of the first edition, but the jigsaw of activities and considerations which constitute the manager's life, and in which a balance must be reached.

In the course of our involvement in training courses and seminars, we have often invited farmers and farm managers to construct their own jigsaw of personal and professional objectives, offering the one shown in Fig. 3.1 as a stimulant to their own thinking.

It has been our experience that this exercise can help the individual to recognize the complexity of his or her personal world, paving the way for a more formal statement of broad objectives and their subsequent quantification. It is, of course, a fact that each individual has to find his or her own answer to the jigsaw and that the pieces of the jigsaw, their relative sizes and their relationship to each other will change with progress through life. Initially, professional ambitions and pride may well dominate, and, while there may be no time in any farmer's life when maximum profit or income

Fig. 3.1. The jigsaw of personal and professional objectives.

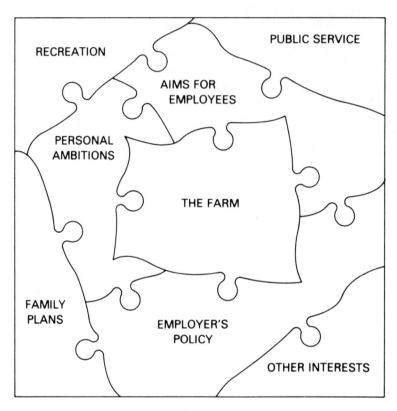

is not an important objective, it is very likely that it will be an especially important driving force during the first half of his or her career. However, the incentive to stretch oneself, simply to increase income, can usually be expected to diminish beyond a certain point and age. The hoary argument that this makes farming primarily a way of life and not a business we regard as a tedious irrelevance. Farming, of course, is both. So are most other businesses to those who manage and work in them, and there is little point in farmers regarding their businesses as in some way different from those of the rest of the economy in this respect.

What is true for everybody, is that reconciling personal, domestic and family considerations with a desire to succeed professionally is an imprecise exercise. Setting objectives smacks of quantification and it is true that short- and long-term business plans can and should be quantified as far as possible. Management by objectives invites that approach. What is also true is that at the more personal level very little can or needs to be quantified in the same way. Finding the right blend between these two areas of life is, however, an important part of any manager's lifestyle. Inevitably there will be conflict. The balance will change, at different times of his or her life, adding to the frustrations involved in setting objectives. It is an uneven job. Parts of it can be quantified and parts cannot be, but it is a situation that must be recognized, thought about and lived with.

Our experience has been that something like the MBO approach – for which our jigsaw is merely a forerunner – can provide the discipline that may be essential if the whole matter is not to be swept under the carpet. The reader may be encouraged to know that when, in training situations, we have invited farmers working in pairs to provide the necessary discipline and stimulation to thought, clear individual objectives have emerged without difficulty – often to the surprise and satisfaction of those concerned. Almost without exception these objectives are, initially, fairly general and vaguely stated. They often have much in common with each other and typical examples include:

- to make a good or adequate profit
- to allow the business to grow
- to keep the farm tidy and good to look at
- to achieve levels of performance in individual enterprises of which we can be proud
- to provide good working conditions for staff
- to keep better records
- to have better communications with my employer
- to spend more time with the family
- to make time for a hobby or personal interest.

Presented with these fairly general statements it is our habit to invite our tutees to go back to the drawing board and quantify their list of objectives in whatever way they can by reference to numerical amounts, time, weights, frequency and type of events, etc. Again, to their surprise, they are able to respond to the discipline of the situation and a typically revised, more quantified list, might be as follows:

- to generate a profit of £X,000, or y% on tenants type capital
- to consider the introduction of at least one new enterprise/activity every x years
- to inspect the farm for tidiness once each month and have a planned programme of maintenance
- to achieve gross margins of £X per ha from the cereal enterprise or £Y margin over concentrates per forage hectare from the dairy enterprise
- to initiate monthly staff meetings with an open agenda
- to take immediate steps to employ appropriate secretarial help in order to install and maintain a system of effective management records
- to propose regular (fortnightly?) meetings with employer, or between

members of a family jointly involved in managing the business
- to plan a minimum of two weeks' holiday with the family, plus a minimum of two long weekend breaks with spouse
- to join the local golf club and set aside a regular half day per week for this activity.

We cannot end this chapter without making reference to two more important aspects of this topic. The first is the carrot-and-stick effect of setting clear and specific objectives of the kind listed above. Initially there can be a certain comfort and encouragement from having cleared the decks and charted the course ahead. It is the sort of feeling that follows the preparation of next year's cropping plan or financial budget which are part and parcel of the wider task that we are talking about. Having stated that something is to be achieved can sometimes almost create the belief that it will be achieved. But we know better. For all kinds of reasons, some of them within our control and some of them beyond it, objectives are not always achieved. Indeed, in overall terms, they seldom are. Then the exercise may become more like a stick than a carrot. The comfort of having charted the way ahead changes to the discomfort of having committed oneself and having failed to keep to the chart. Too much disappointment over this should be avoided, as lessons can and should be learned. Care should be taken, for instance, in the staff meetings referred to above, or the meetings between a manager and his employer, to come to well-discussed agreements about what is desirable and possible. Trying to attain the unattainable can be a frustrating business for all concerned. This topic will be returned to in our chapter on control.

Finally, we should mention the question of time. The foregoing comments will have indicated that a serious consideration of objectives – using something like MBO – is not a simple task. It will therefore take time. It is commonly suggested that up to half a dozen sessions of several hours each will be required. That, in itself, will be a deterrent in a business like farming, where there is usually one manager, and the demands on his or her time are legion. It is even more of a deterrent when it is realized that changing circumstances – changes in the external and internal environments, and changes in the manager's situation and experience – will mean that before too long the whole job will have to be repeated. It is by no means a once-and-for-all task. But it should not be neglected for that reason.

SUMMARY AND LIMITATIONS

This chapter, then, has tried to explain what setting objectives is all about. It is a very important job, but it is a difficult one for a variety of reasons. It needs a careful assessment of the opportunities presented to a business by the external environment and an equally careful assessment of the possibilities that the internal resources offer. It requires self-examination. It requires the help of others. It takes time and it will need repeating. But none of these are reasons for not doing it. On the contrary: while it may be important for managers to do things well now in the short term, it is equally important that they think well in the long term.

In all of this, farmers and farm managers are no different from managers in other sectors. When thinking about objectives, they are confronted by the same basic difficulties, and they have the same kinds of financial and personal needs. Each industry – not just farming – does, of course, have its own particular technical and commercial characteristics which need to be taken fully into account when objectives are being thought about and determined. The rest of this book is largely about the consequences of that exercise.

OUR FINAL THOUGHT

Success will not follow just because objectives have been set. It will follow if those objectives are good ones and if, as far as possible, they are then achieved.

QUESTIONS AND EXERCISES

- Draw a jigsaw of your own personal and professional objectives.

- Make a list of your objectives for the next five years.

- Quantify in whatever way you can (e.g. time, money, percentage, weight, frequency, etc.) each of the objectives you have set.

- List the key result areas in your business/enterprise/job, identifying, where appropriate, the current levels of performance expected from each.

- Set up an MBO meeting appropriate to your business/job. (If you last did this more than two years ago, do it again now!)

GUIDE TO FURTHER READING

Boyer, R. S. (1969) Management by Objectives. *Farm Management* 1, No.5, 1–8.
    Written twenty years ago but worth looking at as one of the few published attempts to relate MBO specifically to farming situations.

Drucker, P. F. (1977) *Management* Pan Books Ltd. Chapter 7: Strategies, Objectives, Priorities and Work Assignments.
    Pure Drucker; says it all, in a book you will be pleased to have for other reasons.

Harvey-Jones, J. (1988) *Making It Happen.* William Collins, London; also (1989) Fontana, London. Chapter 2: Setting the Directions.
    Captures the flavour of this subject in a very readable way.

Humble, J. W. (1972) *Improving Business Results.* McGraw-Hill, London; Pan Books, London.
    Described as 'the definitive work' on MBO, but well within two evenings' pleasant reading. Interesting case-studies included, the essence of which does not date.

Kiam, V. (1986) *Going For It!* Collins, London. Chapter 1: Facing Yourself; finding the entrepreneur in you.
    May be just what you need.

Nicholson, J. H. (1983) MBO Re-considered. *Farm Management* 5, No.2.

Townsend, R. (1970) *Up the Organisation.* Michael Joseph Ltd, London; also (1971) Coronet Books, London.
    Don't deny yourself the pleasure of reading this book. Worth having, if only for the section on objectives – but for many other sections as well.

Chapter 4

Planning

Objectives and plans
The nature of planning
Planning horizons
So what is planning?
Planning within the farm business
— Planning production
— Financial planning
— Planning marketing
— Planning employment

OBJECTIVES AND PLANS

Some readers may feel that this chapter is inseparable from the previous one and in many respects they are right. Some aspects of planning, such as drawing up long-term strategic plans, follow on from any consideration of overall goals and objectives. In this sense, planning, like the setting of objectives, is an integral part of overall management and not a peripheral one. Success will not follow simply from objectives having been set. It will depend on how good, in the business sense of the word, those objectives prove to be, on how effectively they are translated into plans and, finally, on how well those plans are carried out.

We therefore see planning as closely related to objective setting, but separated from it. We also see the concept of planning as having several different connotations which need to be discussed. Therefore, the first part of this chapter examines the nature of planning and is followed by some examples of planning in farm situations.

THE NATURE OF PLANNING

First, we should be quite clear what we mean when we use the word 'plan'. It is commonly defined in dictionaries as 'to arrange beforehand'. In other words it means to give time to something before it happens in order to have some influence over events when they happen. As managers, we should remember that. We wish to have some control over events, rather than let events control us. It is unlikely that we will ever be completely successful in this aim but it is not an unreasonable one to have. Managers are, after all, supposed to manage. Too often we may say, conversationally, that we *plan* to do something when what we really mean is that we *intend* to do it. The real meaning of planning is worth remembering. It requires that time should be given to events before they happen. It is the principal way in which the careful manager avoids what is popularly known as 'management by crisis' – the situations in which managers spend their time and energies responding to things that have gone wrong. By contrast, managers who spend time planning try to anticipate difficulties and mistakes – and certainly to learn from them when they occur – so that future events are less stressful and more successful.

There are several other important characteristics of planning which need emphasis. First, it should not be thought that planning relates solely – or even primarily – to the production process in its limited technical sense. In farm management circles planning has often in fact become synonymous with farm planning, i.e. with choosing a combination of enterprises and devising the annual cropping and stocking programme. This is unfortunate, although it is true that most of the recognizable planning techniques have been applied to this aspect of farm management. However, remembering our definition of planning – to arrange beforehand – it will be obvious to the reader that the process is important across the whole range of management problems and certainly across the four sectors of a business that we identified in our diagrammatic view of management in the second chapter. It may be just as important to spend time planning such matters as the cash flow for the next six months, or the recruitment of a new member of staff, or the marketing of some particular commodity, as it is to spend time on the farm cropping plan. Indeed, important as the farm plan undoubtedly is, there are many other aspects of management, similar to those just mentioned, that will need more constant attention, and at less predictable intervals, than the farm plan, if management by crisis is really to be avoided and if the best possible returns are to be derived from each of the inevitably limited resources which make up any farm business. We will return to this particular economic notion later in the book.

PLANNING HORIZONS

Planning, however, is not only necessary across a wide range of management issues, but also across a wide range of time horizons. As already noted, plans may be closely related to long-term objective setting, making use of well established methods of financial budgeting. Plans of this kind may stretch tentatively ahead for several years, spelling out the approximate path to be followed, or they may contain much more detail, and relate to the farming year ahead. They may relate to a specific operation or innovation such as the installation of a new piece of machinery or the introduction into the system of a new enterprise. Or again, plans may relate to some routine farming operation, such as the annual harvest, or simply to a day's work for an individual, involving perhaps a collection of different jobs all of which need to be completed and must be fitted into a limited period of time.

The overall sequence of planning therefore – moving from long-term strategies through to day-to-day operations, might look something like the diagram in Fig. 4.1.

At any particular time, of course, the farm manager may become involved in any aspect of this overall time horizon without always going back to the beginning or following the whole sequence through. He would get no thanks, for instance, for hesitating in dealing with an immediate problem while he rethinks long-term strategy! Equally, thinking about long-term strategies does not lead to immediate translation into action in the fields.

It is our experience, however, that an appreciation of the different stages in the whole planning horizon – with subsequent identity of the real priorities at any particular point of time – can have far reaching benefit. A little time, (and it may not have to be much), spent towards the end of each day planning the next one, or towards the end of each week, month or season, planning the next one, can be time well spent. Having the peace of mind that stems from a plan helps to allow flexibility with which to cope with unforeseen events.

SO WHAT IS PLANNING?

It follows from this discussion that planning is not synonymous with production planning nor, usually, with sophisticated planning techniques. Such techniques are sometimes needed and can be used with advantage, especially in the production and financial sectors of management. They will be referred to again in the chapters dealing with those topics. It will be clear, however, from the range of management situations mentioned here, and which at some time or another require a planning input, that what is

Fig. 4.1. The sequence of planning.

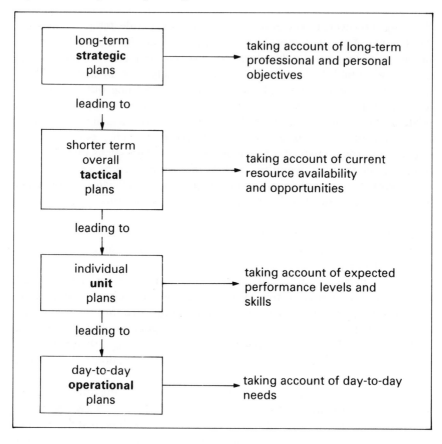

needed may often be no more than an ordered consideration of the facts and possibilities involved. We believe that everyday human attributes such as thoroughness, orderliness and that indefinable thing called 'judgement' will usually play a major part in the process.

Two other important aspects of planning should be mentioned. First, there are many situations in which managers will not find themselves planning from scratch. Plans, however derived, usually already exist; cropping programmes are in being; labour forces exist; capital has already been invested. More often than not, therefore, plans relate to changes and adjustments to existing plans and the scope for adjustment will be constrained by what already exists. It would be convenient if we could always start with a clean slate, but that is seldom the case. This explains why, of all the existing financial planning tools, the partial budget – designed to assess the effect of change – is still the most frequently needed and used. We will deal with it, specifically, in due course.

Secondly, if there is one fact that is common to most plans, it is that, more often than not, they will not work out exactly as they were planned. The failure of a plan in this sense may or may not matter depending on the particular circumstances. What does matter is that the reasons for failure are understood and that lessons for the future are learned. In this sense a failed plan can sometimes teach us more than one which works out entirely as expected. Furthermore, the failure of some plans is certainly not an argument for not planning or budgeting. All planning is, by definition, about future events. When we plan we are trying either to predict or to arrange what will happen in the future. But we cannot know what will happen in the future. In the financial context this is especially true during periods of rapidly changing prices and costs. Past trends and current levels then become a less reliable guide to the future and there may be a strong temptation not to plan, not to budget and perhaps not to change anything. This could be a mistake. It can be argued that it is because of uncertainty that planning is necessary and that increased uncertainty calls for more planning rather than less. There may often be a need for a range of budgets, each making different assumptions about possible changes in the key variables (e.g. yields, prices) which will indicate how sensitive the farm business may be to particular directions and levels of change.

It should however be remembered that while it may be easy to change nothing, it is in fact impossible in any situation literally to do nothing. To do nothing is to do something. It is to go on doing what you have been doing; to commit your present plans and policies to tomorrow's (unknown) prices and costs. Profits, in fact, are the reward for accepting the risks that accompany uncertainty and careful planning is one way in which managers learn to respond to uncertainty. Caution there may need to be, but it could be dangerous to become so mesmerized by uncertainty as to reject all possibility of change.

It will be appreciated from what has been written so far in this chapter that planning is a wide-ranging concept. There are many different aspects of managing a farm business, embracing different time horizons, which demand planning. It will call for care and it will often not be easy. On both these counts it will, therefore, require time. Such evidence as exists in this country on how farmers and farm managers spend their time suggests that planning tends to receive relatively little of it; on average, but obviously depending on the size and nature of the business, about 8%. We would be surprised if the situation was vastly different in other countries. We would agree that forward planning should not become so important as to undermine the need to do today's job well; the future, indeed, may depend on that. But it must also depend on an intelligent anticipation of future events. That is what planning is about.

PLANNING WITHIN THE FARM BUSINESS

There now follow examples of how planning can be used in each of the four main sectors of a business that we have identified: production, marketing, financing and staffing. These examples are of actual farming situations known to us. They have not been presented in order to demonstrate the detailed working out of plans, and certainly not to provide precise answers to the particular situations. They are intended to demonstrate simply the broad spectrum across which planning is necessary and the kinds of consideration that must be incorporated into that process.

Planning production

Since the introduction of milk quotas within the EC in 1984, dairy farmers, in order to maintain their incomes, have found it essential to increase the efficiency of production, involving the need to plan and operate an optimum system for the individual farm, especially in respect of the calving season.

The Milk Marketing Board of England and Wales, faced with the lowering of the absolute level of production coupled with the trend over the 1980s for many producers to change calving patterns towards the autumn, finds mid-summer supplies insufficient for vital needs. Price incentives are therefore being offered for milk produced in July to October in order to obtain a more even profile of supply. This example considers the factors that have to be considered in responding to this incentive by a producer planning to change the emphasis from autumn to summer calving.

The physical difficulty and cost of undertaking such a change needs to be recognized at the outset. Allowing March or April calvers to 'slip' to June is expensive in lost milk and calf income, as is delaying the calving of heifers from the optimum age of two years. Movement in calving needs therefore to be in a forward direction, serving cows after only 6 weeks of lactation and calving heifers at 22-23 months of age. It will therefore take 3-4 years to make a marked influence upon the calving pattern of a herd.

The benefits of summer calving are numerous:

- Cows calve at grass in clean conditions.
- Heifer calves are easy to rear; they are not put to pasture until they are 9 months old so have a better appetite and growth potential.
- Calf prices tend to be above average due to minimal supply.
- Summer mastitis is reduced as there are fewer dry cows in the vulnerable 'fly season'.

- Lactation can be terminated before spring turnout enabling a high stocking density of dry cows and more grass available for conservation.
- Cull cows tend to leave the herd in late winter and so coincide with peak prices.
- June-July calvers require service in August-September when heat observation is easier than in winter. Cows also tend to conceive better at this time.
- Quota management is assisted, as late lactation coincides with the end of the quota year in March, so early drying off can be undertaken with minimal cost.

The major disadvantage is the need to provide adequate supplies of good quality forage to meet the needs of summer calvers. Others are:

- Housing takes place earlier in the autumn with the associated introduction of full winter rations and need for higher silage stocks.
- Silage may also be required for buffer feeding the freshly-calved animals, so that at least 12 tonnes per cow is required annually for a Holstein/Friesian type cow.
- Nitrogen applications to grassland need to be concentrated more towards mid-season to stimulate growth at this time so reducing the response which is highest in spring.
- Spring reseeds or specially sown forage crops may have to be grown to meet feed requirements.
- Nutrition and management of heifers needs to be at a high level to enable trouble-free calving at less than 24 months of age.
- Leave taken by staff during school summer holidays could coincide with the busy calving period.

Computer models based on a cow with 5,000 litre milk sales, under average management and with current milk and feed prices, demonstrate that the highest margin is obtained from mid-summer calving.

Financial planning

Planning the financial aspects of a business can be a considerable challenge to management, especially in respect of an enterprise such as pig production where the future economic environment is particularly uncertain. The manager of a finishing enterprise producing 12,000 baconers per year was recently faced with such a difficult planning exercise. The liquid feeding system, after 15 years of satisfactory performance, began to cause problems, both with the mixing-pumping mechanism and with the mechanical control. Replacement of the unit in such a large enterprise would at first sight appear the obvious course, but many other factors had to be considered.

The problems arose at a critical time when pig meat prices had been severely depressed for over eighteen months, with gross margins dropping to the point where they barely covered labour and electricity costs. The owners – a large farming company – were understandably giving serious consideration to the closure of the unit. The buildings, constructed over a period of twenty years, were in fair condition, but if the unit was to continue in operation for many more years, then major refurbishment would be required.

Good weaner pigs were being purchased from a relatively newly established and well managed outdoor unit with a high health status which was enabling it to stay in business. The bacon pigs were marketed through a most efficient local producer group, with a high proportion of the output being sold to one large multiple who appreciated the quality of the pigs and the service provided by the group. At least the farm had been able to move all the pigs to slaughter at the optimum time during the period when the market was oversupplied.

On seeking quotations for the cost of replacing the faulty parts of the liquid feeder, the manager was concerned to find that these were no longer available. A new improved design had been developed incorporating computerized control, which if linked to a batch pig weigher, could monitor both output and input, so greatly assisting control management.

The cost of the mixer and computer would be £20,000, but with a new weigher and erection of a 'dry' office for the computer unit, the total cost would be nearer £25,000. On receiving this information, the owners were even nearer to making a decision to close the unit!

Advertising material for the new system indicated numerous advantages which the manager studied in detail:

- Feed would be mixed on a weight rather than volume basis so increasing the accuracy of the rations.
- Total feed and ingredient usage, along with its cost, could be recorded.
- Feed cost per animal, food conversion, daily gain and cost per kg gain, could all be readily calculated and displayed on the VDU.
- When fed with appropriate information, the programme could

calculate and display the total weight sold, the average baconer weight and the percentage mortality.

- If pigs could be identified from batch to abattoir and to payment sheet, then profit (or loss) from each batch could also be produced on the screen or on a print-out.

The manager then undertook some fairly simple calculations based upon annual cost of the new unit, to quantify what savings in production cost would be needed to justify the capital sum.

Capital cost	£25,000
Depreciation (5 years)	£5,000
Interest at 16% (on half the sum)	£2,000
Annual cost	£7,000
Cost per pig (12,000 throughput)	£0.60
Current cost of feed per pig in finishing unit	£30
%decrease in feed cost to recoup 60p/pig	2%

The improved accuracy of feed mixing was expected to save 3–4% of feed costs but other gains were also expected. The manager was aware that if the pigs were penned by sex as well as size, the sophistication of the control mechanism would allow differential rationing so that the boars could be finished earlier and at heavier weights than the gilts, but still grade satisfactorily.

On this basis (and with the hope that pigmeat prices would soon improve) a purchase was made. Physical and financial performance improved within weeks of installation and the staff who had been appropriately briefed on the operation of the feeder by the manufacturers, soon gained confidence in using the full potential of the programme.

Pigmeat prices fortunately did improve but the time taken to plan the financial implications of such an investment was well justified and the new unit was effectively written-off in the first year of operation.

Planning marketing

The production of beef from young bulls is an example of a farm enterprise where the financial returns are very much dependent upon the establishment and maintenance of a satisfactory market outlet for the product. Traditionally in the UK, the only bulls processed by the meat trade have been used for breeding purposes and have therefore produced carcasses with a tendency to be tough, dark-coloured and often with an unacceptable taint. The producers of bull beef from young, intensively fed animals had therefore a difficult initial task proving to the buyers that their product was very different and that it really did meet modern customer requirements. This has now been largely overcome and an increasing proportion of beef production is of this type.

The advantages to the producer of leaving his cattle entire are largely in terms of improved growth rate and feed conversion efficiency. In addition, he should expect a premium price as the carcasses produce a higher proportion of saleable meat than is obtained from steers. The product is lean and tender but is usually slightly darker in colour than steer or heifer beef.

There are some disadvantages in operating a beef unit with entire bulls. These include:

- Strong penning and handling areas are essential, which need to be approved by the Health and Safety Executive.
- Cattle have to be fed and bedded without staff entering the pens.
- Two people must be on duty at all times when cattle are handled.
- A sick animal which needs to be taken out of a pen for treatment cannot be returned to the same pen due to bullying. It can perhaps join a group of smaller animals.

Problems can also arise in transportation and at the abattoirs, which lead to excess leanness or dark flesh and rejection by the butcher. Planning is therefore essential at all stages in order to ensure an acceptable product which also justifies a premium price.

As soon as a retail outlet has satisfactorily introduced bull beef to its customers, continuity of supply is of paramount importance. It is harmful to sales to have to change back for short periods to a product with a somewhat different appearance. Communications between the buyer and individual or groups of producers are therefore essential in order to plan long-term supplies. Regular numbers will at times be difficult to provide but an expanding requirement is even more difficult to match as this requires the inputs into production being critically timed. Long-term price agreements are seldom possible, with negotiations related very much to the competition.

The problem of dark-coloured meat is made worse by allowing the bulls to get excited during selection and drafting out of the housing, in transportation and particularly at the abattoirs. Careful planning of all these processes is therefore necessary, with phone calls to check that delivery will be convenient. For initial deliveries it is advantageous for the farmer or stockman to travel with the consignment in order to ensure careful handling at every stage.

On arrival at the abattoirs the bulls should be moved direct to the slaughtering area and not put into lairage where they may come within sight or smell of female cattle. Individual animals within a production group often prove difficult to 'finish', i.e. continue to grow and do not develop sufficient flesh or fatty tissue to produce an acceptable carcass. Such animals need to be sold separately as culls and not allowed to spoil the image of prime quality bull beef.

This example shows the need for on-going communications between producer and purchaser to maintain trust and understanding.

Planning employment

Turning finally to employment, we have the example of a manager of a large arable farm, producing, cereal, beans, and oilseed rape, who, having studied the results of Farm Business costings for his region, was concerned that the fixed costs of his business were significantly above average in respect of both labour and machinery. One of his tractor drivers was approaching retirement but earlier considerations had indicated the need for a replacement, as the workload during harvest and autumn drilling would not be manageable with one fewer member in the team.

During the next harvest season, the local machinery dealer, seeking a suitable site to test and demonstrate a newly designed high-output combine for several days, approached the manager for assistance. The huge machine duly arrived and within the hour, was operating in a field of high-yielding wheat with above average quantity of straw, at almost 30 tonnes per hour. It was first driven by the demonstrator from the manufacturers but he was keen for the two combine drivers from the farm to have a go, and they were highly impressed! The grain tank, with a capacity of 8 tonnes, was sufficient to fill a haulage trailer in one empty, so increasing the efficiency of that operation. The combine engine, even on the steeper slopes, had sufficient power to cope, even with a straw chopper in operation.

The manager began to think that if he could justify replacing his two existing combines with one of these new models, then it would be unnecessary to replace his tractor driver on retirement. The two machines would have a good trade-in value as both had been well maintained, one having done three seasons the other five. With out-of-season discounts, the extra capital sum required to purchase the larger unit could be found within the business. The decision was taken and the first harvest season, with one less person and only the one combine, was a considerable success. Due to the long working day, and the need to maintain 100% driver concentration, shift operation was employed. Both drivers serviced the machine together in the early part of the morning using their joint experience from the previous day. When the conditions were appropriate to start cutting, Driver A operated with Driver B grain-carting. At 3 pm they changed tasks; the farm manager acted as relief to each in turn at lunchtime.

Time had been spent prior to the season planning the availability of spare parts, but fortunately few problems were experienced. Harvest was completed earlier than usual so that autumn cultivation and drilling could be undertaken at the optimum time, despite the team having one member fewer.

OUR FINAL THOUGHT

Planning promotes flexibility not rigidity.

QUESTIONS AND EXERCISES

- Select one day-to-day aspect of your business that is unsatisfactory and carefully plan improved procedures.

- Labour and machinery together constitute a major part of the costs on most farms. Looking ahead for the next five years, prepare plans for the optimum use of these resources in your situation.

- Assuming that a 50 hectare block of land, adjacent to your farm, is expected to be available to rent, plan the physical and financial implications of such an expansion to your business.

- Complete a list of these aspects of your business that you feel do not plan sufficiently well. Resolve to tackle these, one by one.

GUIDE TO FURTHER READING

Barnard, C. S. and Nix, J. S. (1979) *Farm Planning and Control* (Second Edition). Cambridge University Press, Cambridge.
    Chapter 1 (The planning environment and the managerial function) is valuable reading in its own right but is essential for those who intend to get more involved in this basic text.

Drucker, P. F. (1967) *Managing for Results.* Heinemann, London. Also Pan Books, London.

Chapter 11 (Making the future today) is salutary comment on a preoccupation with 'tomorrow'.

Humble, J. W. (1972) *Improving Business Results.* Pan Books, London.

Already recommended for the previous chapter, but Part Two is relevant here also.

Nix, J. S. (1969) Annotated bibliography of farm planning and programming techniques. *Farm Management* 1, No. 7.

Could save you a lot of unnecessary reading or researching.

Turner, J. and Taylor, M. (1989) *Applied Farm Management.* BSP Professional Books, Oxford.

Chapters 7–10 concentrate on this aspect of management in various ways.

Chapter 5

Decision-Making

```
The importance of decision-making
         The components
       − identifying the issue
       − assessing significance
      − considering alternatives
      − collecting information
            − evaluation
              − choice
         − implementation
        − checking results
          − responsibility
The importance of judgement and time
        a strategic decision
        a tactical decision
```

THE IMPORTANCE OF DECISION-MAKING

Decision-making has many facets. It may concern the present or the future; it may concern a trivial or a major issue; and the available options may be few or many, quantifiable or not quantifiable. Whatever the circumstances, however, decision-making is characterized by the fact that decisions have to be taken at a particular point in time, based at least in part on information that comes from a previous time, about events that will happen at some future time. Seen in that light, it is seldom an easy process and the description of management as 'the art of making good decisions based on inadequate information from dubious sources' comes close to the truth.

Once again, we come face to face with the inter-relationships between different aspects of management. As we have seen, it is vital to have clear objectives, to devise plans which reflect those objectives and, as we shall see in the next chapter, to try to ensure that things happen as planned. Planning and controlling are linked by the fact that managers take decisions: decisions to do certain things in certain ways. Events actually occur because managers decide that they should occur; without decisions there would, in fact, be no productive activity at all. Probably the reader will agree that whatever other topics are singled out as important elements in the manager's job, decision-making must be amongst them. Some writers on management go so far as to say that it is decision-making, above all else, which characterizes the manager's role; that management is essentially a decision-making activity. We agree on its importance, but we consider that management concerns many other things as well. It is a comprehensive task, as our definition stressed.

In order to make our position quite clear, however, we need to emphasize three particular aspects of decision-making which make it so important. First, the fact that decisions are continually being made; secondly, that they can have a lasting, or at least far-reaching influence on what is achieved; and thirdly, that they can influence how well things are achieved. Let us briefly examine each of these thoughts in turn.

Decisions are continually being made in businesses, if only because something is continually happening. It is easy to identify decision-making with change, with a shift of emphasis or methods. What is equally true is that if events continue unaltered, it is because a decision has been made (albeit automatically or subconsciously) not to change. It is unlikely that the manager of a dairy farm, for instance, consciously decides to go on milking his cows each day; but in effect, each day that he does go on milking them he is allowing capital, labour and management to be employed in this particular way. A considered or subconscious intention to change nothing is therefore a positive action; in economic terms it means to commit present-day resources and plans to tomorrow's prices and costs. Financial outcomes are thus being determined by decisions not to change – or to change – things, as the case may be, and decision-making, in this sense, becomes a continuous part of management.

Turning to the second point that we wish to make here, it is important to be aware of those situations when decisions are being made that will have a far-reaching effect on the future course of a farm business, and then to leave no stone unturned in an endeavour to make 'good' decisions. No more can be expected. There is hardly such a concept as a right decision. Only the outcome of the chosen course of action is ever known. Other possible outcomes – which may have been better, or worse – are never known. Good strategic decisions are therefore what are sought, compatible with long-term objectives and with the constraints and possibilities that should have been built into those objectives. From time to time decisions to abandon an enterprise, to introduce another, or to expand or contract – perhaps even to change farms – will need to be made. They may influence the course of a business and the rewards from it for years ahead; they should not be taken lightly.

Our third point is simply that how enterprises are managed (as opposed to what enterprises are managed) will also have a very important influence on what results are achieved. The significance of technical competence has already been mentioned in an earlier chapter and will be mentioned again in later ones. It cannot be over-stressed. Many day-to-day and week-to-week decisions will have to be made, often in the face of changing weather conditions that certainly do complicate the lives of farm managers in a way that may not affect their counterparts in other parts of the economy. These are the tactical decisions. They must always be made in the context of longer term strategic decisions that will, hopefully, already have been taken. In the long term they will have less significance than strategic decisions about what to do, but in the context of a particular crop, a particular season and a particular year's profit, they can be vital. More often than not such decisions will not relate to a problem as such. It will simply be that a decision between one possible course of action and another, or between several possibilities, has to be taken. Indeed, the need for decision-making at all, comes about only because there is a choice between alternatives. Without choice there is no need for decision, and we should not automatically identify decision-making with problem-solving. Sometimes there will be a genuine problem to be solved; but often we will simply be in the business of selecting between alternatives, which may be equally attractive – or unattractive!

THE COMPONENTS OF DECISION-MAKING

So far we have written in fairly general terms about the importance and nature of decision-making. But what, in fact, does it involve? In this section we try to answer that question by identifying those procedures which managers should – mentally at least – engage in if they are to take their decision-making seriously. We are not suggesting that in every situation and wherever a choice of any kind has to be made, one will, or should, go through this formal and apparently laborious process. That would be tedious and often unnecessary. Experience, judgement and the familiarity of 'having been here before' help managers to make quick decisions when the situation calls for it – either because the matter is urgent or because it is insufficiently important to warrant any significant input of time. Nevertheless, there are many other more important situations when something like the sequence of thinking that is set out below is required.

Identifying the issue or problem in hand

This may seem so obvious as not to require mention, but we do not want to spend valuable time finding the right answer to the wrong problem, with all the waste of effort and resources which that implies. It is all too easy to be guilty of 'symptomatic diagnosis', as the jargon describes it, clutching at first impressions and failing to go back to the beginning to identify the real problem or issue.

Assessing significance

With the first hurdle overcome, it is important for a busy manager – and what manager is not busy? – to assess the significance of the issue that he or she has now identified. How important is this issue in terms of capital commitment, profit potential, morale of staff and influence on other activities and possibilities, and how irreversible would a wrong decision be? In short, how much time does it deserve, and whose time does it deserve? The more significant the issue about which a decision is required, the more important is the involvement of senior management.

Senior managers, aware as they should be of all the circumstances surrounding a particular decision, must constantly be prepared to determine priorities – a topic we shall consider later in the book. Considering significance, in this way, will help a manager to allocate his or her efforts appropriately and determine how formal and how involved he or she needs to be in reaching a decision in the area in question.

Considering alternatives

Assuming that the issue has been identified and judged to be significant, a careful consideration of the possible alternative courses of action should be embarked on. At this stage it is important to keep an open mind, to consult and discuss as widely as possible – inside and outside the business – and not to 'close the book' too hastily. At the beginning it is better to have many choices than few; discussion and reflection will then serve to narrow down the real possibilities. It is our experience that too hasty decisions can sometimes be made simply because inadequate time has been devoted to this aspect of the decision-making process.

In what may at first sight, for instance, be a fairly simple decision about how to sell a particular crop or bunch of livestock, careful consideration of the alternatives may reveal a much wider range of real possibilities than was first envisaged. It may then be necessary, simply to make the task manageable, gradually to narrow the choice down to something like the four

options shown in Fig. 5.1, for each of which detailed information must then
be assembled and evaluated before a rational choice can be made.

Collecting information

This will be an essential next part of the procedure. What is wanted here
will be partly determined by the kind of evaluation that is subsequently
envisaged. All of the normal rules about budgeting will apply. Reliable
physical data allied to the best possible estimates of future prices and costs
is needed; muster all the accuracy that you possibly can. The task will not
be easy, especially if activities are being contemplated that are new to the
business concerned. If that is the case, it must be remembered that case
study and experimental data can be a poor guide to commercial operation
on *your* farm under *your* management. Remember also that 'over the
fence' impressions and verbal accounts of results from neighbours and
associates can – with no intent to mislead – be less than the whole truth.
Real communication at this level can be elusive. It is also important, even
in situations where quantitative evaluation is possible, that non-quantitative
information should also be sought. The effect of possible changes in
patterns of production on such matters as ease of organization, personal
strain, and quality control may be important considerations. Getting reliable facts, before they become part of your own history, requires careful
research and later on we devote a whole chapter to that aspect of management, while some of the intricacies of piecing information together in
budgetary form are discussed in the next paragraph.

Fig. 5.1. Considering the alternatives.

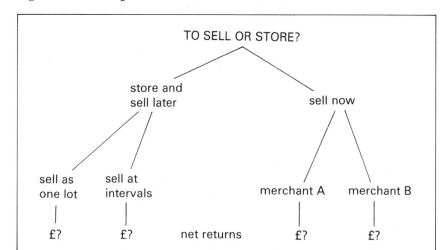

Evaluation

Not all decision-making situations will lead to the point where numerical evaluation is necessary, although by definition some judgement will always be required in the light of the issue in hand, the options that are open and whatever information about those options can be gleaned. Where, however, numerical evaluation is both indicated and possible, it is our firm belief that the time-honoured partial budget (what extra income and cost and what avoided income and cost is involved?) is the most simple, effective and, therefore, appropriate management tool to use. Managers are well advised to become adept in its use – and the pocket calculator should never be far away! The partial budget is essentially concerned with changes in profitability and will need to be interpreted in the light of other non-numerical considerations. Where investment is involved – and some capital appraisal is required – the partial budget can lead on to a simple calculation of the percentage return of the extra profit on the amount of fresh capital required to generate it. This is known as the rate of return. Alternatively, omitting any depreciation element from the budget, an estimate can be made of how quickly the investment will be recouped; this is the 'pay back' method. With outside specialist help, more sophisticated evaluation methods and operational research techniques may be used, but we believe that for many cases the simple approach, applied by the manager alone, has advantages. Some of these approaches will be returned to again in our final chapter, whilst the relevant chapters in the farm management books recommended as further reading provide more detailed illustration of the techniques than we have offered.

Choice

Sooner or later will come the moment of decision. A choice will have to be made, even if it is to do nothing. Very often the actual moment of decision may be difficult to recognize; a consensus of opinion tends to develop in the face of economic and other evidence, so that a good decision emerges. This will usually suggest that sound preliminary work has been done at the sifting and evaluation stage. Time and facts have eliminated the non-starters. At other times there will be more agony. Non-quantitative considerations then, perhaps, become more important. Judgement and experience take over from calculations and some managers, of course, become more adept in these matters than others.

Implementation

A decision taken must then be acted upon; the decision must be properly communicated to those responsible for its implementation. It may be a simple internal matter involving one or more persons, or a major development involving professional and commercial interests outside the farm business. Sequencing of events will then become important and we are back in the realms of planning.

Checking results

Decisions are taken because certain desired results are anticipated. These may not always occur. What happens as a result of a decision should be monitored – numerically or otherwise – and checked against expectations. Faults should be corrected as quickly as possible before events drift permanently off track. But now we are into another major realm of business management, namely that of control, to which we will turn in the next chapter.

Responsibility

Finally, whether a decision proves to have been a good one or not, management must be prepared to take responsibility for it. Hopefully, appropriate consultation within an organization will have taken place at all stages. Decisions may or may not have emerged by mutual agreement and consensus, but responsibility for the final moment of decision and its implementation rests fairly and squarely with management. That is one of the things that managers are paid for. If a good decision has been made they can enjoy the knowledge that they inspired it; if it has not, they shoulder the blame.

THE IMPORTANCE OF JUDGEMENT AND TIME

Before going on to illustrate the application of this systematic approach to decision-making we wish to say a final word on the importance of 'judgement' and 'time'. It will be clear to the reader that although numerical techniques can play an important part in the overall process that has just been described – especially in dealing with alternative courses of action and their evaluation – there are other aspects of the process which rely very much more on subjective assessment using experience and judgement. In our estimation, judgement is an important quality in all aspects of management.

Although not easy to define it is a word that we wish to stress. In the decision-making process it is especially important in recognizing the issue and in selecting the preferred course of action. It is at the all-important beginning and end of the process that the ability to exercise judgement plays its part, preparing the way for evaluation and interpreting the results. Computers of one sort or another may play an important part in 'evaluation' but they cannot replace the judgement that must be displayed by the manager himself.

We believe that, closely related to a manager's ability to exercise judgement, are the ability to recognize when a particular matter deserves his time, and the willingness to give it. Often during the course of the working day or week quick decisions are needed. Good managers will learn when such decisions can safely be made and when they cannot be. As a general rule, staff will be frustrated by a manager who hesitates unreasonably when tactical decisions are needed. Hasty decisions should not be made in the strategic situations referred to earlier, especially when significant amounts of capital are involved, or when for any other reason, including the safety of employees, situations are not easily and cheaply reversible. A good rule of thumb may be: can this decision be quickly and cheaply reversed? When the answer is 'no' it is important for managers to give, without unnecessary delay, that amount of time to decision-making which leaves them as confident as they can be that their decision has been a good one – and may even have been the right one.

EXAMPLE OF A STRATEGIC DECISION

The decision to introduce a system of complete diet feeding (CDF) to a dairy herd is taken to illustrate a complex decision involving not only the feeding of cows but also the management and organization of a dairy enterprise. The system involves mixing forages, concentrates and other constituents of a diet in a specialized mixer-feeder trailer which is fitted with a weighing mechanism; the ration is then dispensed to a group of cows which has constant access to the manger except at milking times. Feeding during milking can be eliminated, and intake of an individual cow is determined by her appetite and by management decisions as to which group she belongs to and the composition of the diets. There are many physical, nutritional and financial considerations to be taken into account before making a decision to introduce CDF but a systematic approach can be seen to be of value.

Identifying the issue

This system of feeding dairy cattle can be looked upon as being applicable especially to a large herd situation where high yields and margins are being achieved. The capital cost of the mixer-feeder alone is a considerable sum but if building modifications are necessary to store ingredients or to provide mangers then herd performance is of major importance. There is no magic associated with the machine, as the diets produced are only as good as the ingredients used, so that if a dairy farmer is dissatisfied with the current herd performance, he should identify and correct any shortcomings before contemplating CDF. Key factors in the profitability of dairy farming include the availability of high quality forage together with skilled and dedicated herdsmanship. These factors are also essential to successful CDF and the system can be best looked upon as one which can help the good to become even better.

Assessing significance

A number of high performance dairy units have, in recent years, undergone a logical sequence of changes in the way in which cows have been fed and managed. Self-feeding of silage has been replaced by mechanical handling of precision-chopped material fed in mangers. As well as feeding concentrates at milking time, one or more additional feeds have been introduced outside the parlour to spread intake and help rumen digestion. To a dairy farmer who has followed this pattern of development, CDF is the next logical step. He will need only to replace the normal forage box with a mixer-feeder and can also avoid the cost of parlour feeders as and when they need replacement. He will need to assess at this stage, the effect of the system on his staff in terms of skills, training and motivation.

Considering alternatives

There are several feasible alternative systems of feeding a large high-yielding herd which justify serious consideration:

1. Mixing complete diets without the purchase of a specialized machine, by adding food ingredients in layers into a forage box or converted manure spreader. These machines take longer to fill, they do not usually have a weighing device and the standard of mix is less satisfactory.
2. Feeding of forages and concentrates as normal at milking time but providing additional concentrates from cow-activated automatic dispensers located in the housing areas. Development of these out-of-parlour units

continues but as the level of sophistication increases so does the cost, which is equal to or greater than that of CDF machinery. One major snag of these feeders that has been pinpointed by behavioural studies is the wide variability of use by individual cows within the herd.

3. Automatic dispensing of concentrates to every cow from a timed augering device in the front of the cubicles. This system, although considerably more expensive in initial cost and in maintenance, requires a low labour input. It is a possible alternative in a building layout which does not provide satisfactory space for mangers or access for feeding vehicles.

Collecting information

We have indicated in the early part of this chapter that this is often an important factor in decision-making and it is especially so with this example. Although a few machines have been operating in the UK for several years, widespread interest in CDF is more recent. The feeding of a dairy cow is also a long-term consideration: a change in nutrition may well affect milk output in the short term, but it also has a longer term effect upon milk quality, cow weight, condition and conception rate. The common practice in farming, to ask a neighbour how he is getting on with his new machine, is not always the ideal way to obtain an unbiased opinion. It is only natural for a person who has made the decision to spend a large capital sum to see more clearly the advantages and to be hopeful that any snags are temporary. Fortunately, not all farmers react in this way and reliable information can be obtained from users, often through contacts such as ADAS machinery advisers. These users will detail the problems they have experienced in such matters as cows being unwilling to come into the parlour, and animals which on ad-lib feed put on flesh and fat instead of producing milk. The question of summer feeding will arise, including the possibility of employing CDF throughout the year or using the machine to buffer grazing with other types of feed.

Evaluation

Numerical evaluation is possible here, at least as far as putting a sum to the additional costs that CDF will involve. The capital requirement will be known, so that taking depreciation, interest, maintenance and repairs, an annual charge can be calculated. Labour costs will seldom be included in the calculation as a change to CDF should not alter the number of staff employed, although in some situations overtime payments may be affected. Cost per animal will be markedly reduced if the machinery can also be used to service a heifer-rearing or a beef unit on the same farm. Several dairy herds can also be fed using one machine if travelling distance is reasonable or if manger capacity allows alternate day filling. The calculation of the benefits is a more difficult area. Some savings in cost may well be obtained, e.g. the price of concentrates bulk-tipped compared to the same material blown into hoppers above a parlour or obtained in sacks for the out-of-parlour feeds. Purchased proprietary concentrates can be replaced by using the machine as a home mixer and buying ingredients on a least-cost basis. Deducing such savings from the additional costs will leave the sum to be covered by increased output if the project is to break even. Some managers may, in a period of marked inflation, be satisfied with breaking even, if they have a system easier for staff to operate and one which can be more satisfactorily controlled from the farm office. Others will require a certain return on the investment and will therefore need to calculate the additional returns required. The difficulty arises in putting a value not just on any additional milk output and compositional quality, but also on such factors as improved conception rate and even change in calving pattern.

Choice

Having followed the factors through in detail to this stage, it should be a relatively clear-cut decision as to whether the system in a particular situation is justified or not. If alternative feeding systems become more attractive in the future, the mixer-feeder trailer could be used as a simple forage dispenser.

Implementation

The successful outcome of the new system is very much dependent upon the way it is implemented. The following steps are necessary:

1. Explain in detail to all staff the likely benefits, and more importantly the expected difficulties. The difficulty of cows entering the parlour could develop into a major problem or be considered as a challenge, depending upon the level of motivation of the stockmen.

2. Arrange a training session for the operators, to be undertaken by the local dealer's or manufacturer's staff.

3. Assemble a supply of appropriate spare parts and make arrangements with the dealer, and perhaps in conjunction with other local users, to ensure availability of an emergency parts service.

4. Prepare a system of information flow from office to feeder and back to enable accurate control.

5. Introduce the diets to the cows over an extended period so as to avoid digestive upset, especially with the high-yielding groups.

Checking results

As well as recording feed dispensed on a daily basis, monthly or even weekly stock checks will be necessary to enable inputs to the herd as a whole to be compared with budgeted figures. Accuracy of feeding to the various groups will depend upon the weighing mechanism of the mixer-feeder so that a periodic check over a weighbridge is a valuable operation. Milk output from each group can be obtained either by taking bulk tank dipstick readings between groups, or ideally by using an in-line flow meter. Cow weights and condition scores will be a useful indicator to the longer term benefits of the new system.

Responsibility

It follows from the previous point that a manager making a decision to introduce CDF may well have to go through a difficult period when the problems are obvious to all but the benefits much less so. Motivation of the staff will be a major factor through this period, but if careful implement-ation is carried out as outlined, few difficulties should arise. This is, in fact, the job of management: to take the decisions and to take the responsibility for them until they reach fruition.

EXAMPLE OF A TACTICAL DECISION

Managers involved in making a strategic decision, as in the previous example, have adequate time in which to carefully consider all the various aspects, and especially to obtain relevant information. Many other farm management decisions, often equally important in terms of financial outcome, have to be made in a much shorter period of time. Some tactical decisions are taken on a daily basis, such as when to cut a ley for hay, while others are 'one-off' decisions dealing with a crisis or unexpected problem. Take, for example, an oilseed rape grower in the South of England who in the first four years of growing the crop has experienced reasonable weather at the harvesting season and so has been able to direct harvest using the farm combines with minimal difficulty.

In year five, the crop looks particularly promising but is somewhat vari-able in maturity. As harvest approaches, the weather is particularly unset-tled and the forecast is of no comfort. In such a tactical decision-making process, there is no time or justification for going through the more formal aspects of the process. The problem is obvious – if the crop is left for direct cutting, a considerable proportion of the seed will no doubt be shed – but the amount is difficult to quantify.

The alternatives are to spray with a desiccant or to arrange for the crop to be swathed. Information must therefore be obtained at once as to the possibility, at such short notice, of a contractor having a swather available: if a machine is available, cost will be a secondary consideration at this late stage. However, the likelihood is that desiccation may have to be seriously considered. Using the farm sprayer and standard tractor may not provide adequate clearance of the spray boom over the crop to achieve adequate coverage and spray penetration. The need for high volume spraying and the benefit of a wide boom to minimize wheel damage again point to contractor equipment. If farm equipment is used and is totally at the manager's disposal, it is best to limit the area desiccated in one day to that which can be safely combined in two days.

With each successive step, timing of the operation is important to success, but at such a late stage of decision-making a compromise may have to be accepted. Next year it may be wise at least to book the services of a contractor, but even then a decision will be needed as to how best to proceed.

OUR FINAL THOUGHT

A good manager learns to recognize when an issue or problem deserves the time that he or she gives it; a hastily made 'right' decision on the wrong question is a bad use of time. Judgement is a key ingredient in the decision-making process.

QUESTIONS AND EXERCISES

- Identify an important decision that you have been deferring. Decide when you are going to take it and how you will go about it – and then take it!

- Consider a 'diversified' enterprise that you might add to your business. Using the decision-making procedure outlined in this chapter, reach a considered view of its feasibility and potential.

- Chapter 3 made reference to conflicting business and personal objectives. In reviewing your own, make decisions about the ranking of priorities for you and your business in the next few years.

- Identify the environmental pressures that are likely to effect your business and decide how best you can accommodate them.

GUIDE TO FURTHER READING

Barnard, C. S. and Nix, J. S. (1979) *Farm Planning and Control.* Cambridge University Press, Cambridge.
Chapters 3 and 14 contain relevant arithmetic.

Drucker, P. F. (1968) *The Practice of Management.* Heinemann, London; also Pan Books, London.
Read Chapter 28; as always Drucker gets first things first.

Hardaker, J. B. (1969) Decision trees: a systematic approach to decision-making under uncertainty. *Farm Management Notes* No. **39**, 9–18. Dept. of Agricultural Economics, University of Nottingham.
A numerical but understandable and helpful guide to the decision-maker who, even if he or she makes 'sweeping simplifications' and constructs 'a crude decision tree' will have 'a better understanding of the choices he faces and of the risks he must bear'.

Norman, L., Turner, R. and Wilson, K. (1985). *The Farm Business.* Longman, London.
Chapters 2 and 5 contain relevant arithmetic.

Turner, J. and Taylor, M. (1989) *Applied Farm Management.* BSP Professional Books, Oxford.
Chapter 1 makes general references to the decision-making procedure and indicates where else in the book examples are given.

Chapter 6

Control

The importance of control
The essence of control
The nature of targets
Applications to farming
Monitoring the whole business
Short period enterprise checks
Short period input checks
Inability to control
Control at the heart of matters

THE IMPORTANCE OF CONTROL

We have already stated that we are reluctant to think in terms of one topic being more important than any other in management, but if pressed, the need for effective control would come high on our list of priorities. Let us explain why.

We single out three reasons for attaching so much importance to this topic. First, because it is concerned with actually doing what is intended; secondly, because it is a continuous requirement; and thirdly, because without some form of control system, inadequate performance can easily be masked in any multi-enterprise business.

The first of these three reasons hardly needs elaboration, but may easily be overlooked. A moment's thought, however, will make it obvious that if careful thought and precious time have been invested into all those aspects of management that have been discussed in the previous three chapters – setting objectives, making plans, and taking decisions in order to put those plans into operation – then a good deal of that thought and time will have been wasted if events are simply allowed to take care of themselves; if, in fact, events control management rather than the other way round. It is a simple message, but one not to be ignored. It really is important that,

58

insofar as external influences permit, events work out as they were intended to. Otherwise, why bother to plan?

The second important point about control is that the need for it is so continuous. Farmers and farm managers do not need to spend vast amounts of time thinking about setting objectives, although they should always keep the objectives they have set themselves well to the front of their minds; nor do they spend large amounts of time drawing up plans, although they may often be turning their plans over in their mind; and nor are they, despite what has been written about the subject in the previous chapter, making decisions all day long. They are, however, concerned all the time with operations being done properly, with timeliness, with care and with the correct applications of technical know-how. If, as it is often claimed, many farm managers are more at home out on the farm than they are in their offices, then control should not be an alien function to them. It is, in fact, what much of practical farming is about; making sure that, in a physical sense, the right things are done in the right way, by the right people, and especially important, at the right time. It is the most continual part of the farm manager's job.

Thirdly, and lastly, we regard an effective control system as very important if there is any danger at all of poor technical or economic performance being 'masked' by good performance elsewhere and therefore left undetected. In farming this can very easily happen. We are not being critical if we observe that the number of farmers who farm without a detailed budget is large, even in the 1990s, many years after farm business management first took root as a formal discipline. This can easily mean that profit targets are unrelated to carefully thought out statements of what is likely to happen and what is reasonable and instead reflect a more or less enlightened expectation of what the overall financial outcome might be, based on what has happened in the past, mentally adjusted for the effect of changing prices and costs. Sometimes such estimates can be close to the mark – but sometimes not! In any event, such an approach offers no useful guide as to what in detail ought to have happened in each sector of the farm, or in each of the main cost centres. The ease with which one miscalculation can compensate for another can be frightening. Indeed, the situation in which an overall profit target is achieved without a detailed calculation as to how it should have been or was achieved may be more dangerous in terms of undetected and therefore uncorrected defects, than that in which the target is not met. In the latter case, at least there will be no delusion and investigation is likely to follow. It is still the case that despite moves towards simple and more specialized farming systems, most farms comprise a number of different enterprises, and several of the more important farm costs (e.g. labour and machinery) are shared between those enterprises. Final profits, therefore, usually stem from a good deal of interlocking of activities with the obvious possibility of the efficient compensating for the inefficient. It is a dangerous situation which is especially common in agriculture and requires careful monitoring. It is one of the main reasons why we regard control as of such importance.

THE ESSENCE OF CONTROL

Before going on to discuss the application of control systems to farming, it is important that we should be quite clear about what is involved. It is not a complicated concept although some confusion might arise because of the two levels at which the subject exists. There is, at the practical work-a-day level, the physical performance of tasks. It needs control and so does the supervision of the staff involved. This aspect of control is concerned with getting things done. But there is also the question of the end result, both in physical and in financial terms, and measurement against a target. In other industries this approach is known as budgetary control, and it has gradually obtained acceptance in farming. It is an office job, not an open air one.

Although these two aspects of control are widely separated in terms of when they occur and how often they occur, we prefer not to make too wide a distinction between them. They are both part of the same basic need to try to control events and physical performance interacts with the financial appraisal. Both parts of the job entail the following steps:

- Having a target in mind
- Knowing how you intend to set about achieving it
- Knowing what, in the event, you do achieve
- Relating achievement to the target
- Understanding the magnitude and reasons for any divergence between the two (in whatever direction)
- Taking corrective action, as soon as possible, wherever it is necessary
- Reviewing and, if necessary, adjusting targets for the next production cycle.

THE NATURE OF TARGETS

The word 'target' has just been used several times and it is worth considering the nature of these targets. Some farmers and managers with whom we have discussed this matter over the years have not been clear about this at all. They have often thought of targets as being something to aim at which should, therefore, be at least slightly beyond reach. In our view, in the context of budgetary control, physical targets and financial budgets should be realistic, based on known levels of performance and related to likely financial prices and costs; they should be attainable. Uncertainty and inflation simply increase the difficulty of the exercise, but they do not remove the need for it. The importance, also, of adequate consultation with staff, as in any consideration of future objectives and plans, should be obvious. Specialist staff may well have insights, often denied to overall managers, into what is possible within their enterprise and what is not. Their contribution should be welcomed and used.

Budgets of a different kind – break even budgets or budgets reflecting what might be achieved given higher levels of performance – have their uses in other contexts. So far as control is concerned, however, budgets should depict simply the best estimate of what is really expected to happen. This does not mean that they are blueprints to be slavishly followed. Opportunities to improve on the budget should obviously be pursued. They will help to compensate for the things that, inevitably, fall short. As we have already acknowledged, few plans work out exactly as planned.

During the farming year, it will sometimes become apparent that initial expectations are either not going to be achieved or going to be exceeded. In this sense the target becomes a moving one. It is then possible and, given the best possible knowledge of what the overall outcome is likely to be, sensible to adjust the budget accordingly. In control terms, however, there is a danger here. If budgets continue to be altered throughout the year, in accordance with changes in physical and financial events, the net result will be that the revised budget is always achieved. There will be no deviation from the plan and, apparently, no need for correction. Our advice in this situation would be to have two budgets; one to be adjusted and one not, and it is against the latter one that the most meaningful comparisons can be made between actual and budgeted performance. It is in the light of that kind of comparison that corrective action can be instigated or future plans and budgets adjusted. The adjustable budget, on the other hand, will be valuable in indicating, at the earliest possible moment, what the eventual outcome of a year's trading is likely to be.

APPLICATIONS TO FARMING

Having now considered the importance of control and the nature of budgetary targets, we can proceed to illustrate in more detail some of the ways in which control techniques can be applied to farming operations.

A full discussion of the technique of preparing budgets will be reserved until our chapter on financial management but it is impossible to discuss control – at least the financial as opposed to the supervisory aspects of it – without some reference to budgets. Frequently they are used to help make decisions between one course of action and another; but here we are concerned with budgets to help exercise control.

In general terms our position on this subject is as follows:

---

1. We regard the two approaches to control already referred to (i.e. supervisory and budgetary) as of equal importance, and, in so far as they should both be about achieving predetermined targets, interacting with each other.
2. Supervisory control can be closely equated with what is known as 'management by walking around', i.e. by inspection and direction.
3. Budgetary control, although involving desk work of one kind or another, is not simply or even primarily about arithmetic – it is about underlying causes of error and, ultimately, about corrective action.
4. Such control can be exercised
    (a) annually and/or in shorter periods over the whole business
    (b) annually and/or in shorter periods over individual enterprises
    (c) annually and/or in shorter periods over individual inputs
       – especially those not incorporated in (b) above.
5. Short period control checks on individual enterprises are most sensibly confined to those items over which some degree of control can in fact be exercised in the short period, e.g. animal feed in the intensive enterprises. Their required frequency will depend on how frequently action can be taken and would differ, therefore, for say a pig fattening enterprise and a traditional beef system.
6. The frequency of short period control checks on inputs is likely to depend on whether the expenditure is of the 'tap' or the 'stream' type – a distinction to be described shortly.

Armed with these general principles we will now examine their application in more detail, concentrating here on the budgetary approach (i.e. on items 4, 5 and 6 above) whilst leaving the supervisory approach to be developed more fully in our staff management chapter. As there is inevitable interaction between the two, let it be noted here that any corrective action that we are seeking, at least in the short period, is likely to centre around the achievement (or not) of physical performance levels. These should have been set on the basis of known past performance and reasonable expectations of the future, and agreed with staff. Close collaboration and discussion with staff – supervision in the way that we envisage it – will be an important ingredient in the endeavour to grow crops, breed and feed livestock and produce livestock products – or to do anything else that, these days, is encompassed within farming businesses.

MONITORING THE WHOLE BUSINESS

In an era when there is (rightly) much emphasis on individual enterprise control checks (especially in the livestock sector) our continued enthusiasm for a check on the whole farm business, carried out at least annually, stems from the possibility of masking, or overlap, referred to at the beginning of this chapter. It is also important to remember that profits are derived from whole businesses and too much emphasis on the bits and pieces, to the exclusion of the whole, could mean that the very cause of failure escapes detection. Seeing the whole picture, therefore, can be very important, although just how much detail is initially embraced in this type of exercise is very much for the individual to decide. Our view has always been that a determination to apply control techniques, in a form which is agreeable to the person undertaking the task, is far more important than the particular method used. We are not purists in these matters and on balance we would settle for something that, in the first instance, helps to identify where major problems may exist; these can then be explored in more detail.

The following single hypothetical situation, for instance, comparing a budget with actual performance on a milk and corn producing farm, at once points to the underlying causes for profit being less than half of the expected level – and would prompt further questioning (and further record keeping) of certain areas of the business (Table 6.1).

In the example of Table 6.1, which uses very rounded figures and has been simplified to illustrate the point, all of the difference between budgeted and actual performance exists in the production element of the business. In our experience this is not unusual with production more in the lap of the gods than costs which, with practice, can often be predicted with considerable accuracy – if not with the precise accuracy suggested in this case! On inspection, of course, it is only the total cost which corresponds to budget; item by item there are several differences which cancel each other out – something that should be carefully watched in case the 'good' covers up the 'bad'. In the event, however, it is the cows that have let things down and, as may often be the case, with many costs of a fixed or fairly fixed nature, all of the deficit comes off the profit.

This illustration has deliberately been presented without great detail. It has the dual merit in our view of being simple and quick to calculate and of indicating where a closer examination is likely to pay dividends. Certainly, where particular problems seem to exist a more detailed approach will be called for, if it does not already exist. Targets will need to be expressed in the appropriate detail and achieved results measured in a similar way. Taking the cows as an example, the situation might look as in Table 6.2.

By comparing the planned and actual amounts of production from each enterprise in this way, it will be possible to assess how much, if any, differ-ence between the two is attributable to: (a) the number of units involved

Table 6.1. Comparison of budget with actual performance for a dairy and arable farm.

	Budget £	Actual £	Difference £
Output			
Crops	64,000	65,000	+1,000
Milk	68,800	57,000	−11,800
Cattle	15,000	14,000	−1,000
Total	147,800	136,000	−11,800
Costs			
Livestock	10,000	9,500	−500
Purchased feed	16,800	16,700	−100
Seed	5,500	5,500	0
Fertilizer	13,800	13,500	−300
Rent	18,600	18,600	0
Power and machinery	27,600	28,000	+400
Labour	21,500	22,500	+1,000
Sundries	16,000	15,500	−500
Total	129,800	129,800	0
Profit	18,000	6,200	−11,800

Table 6.2. Comparison of budget and actual performance for milk production.

	Cows		Milk		Price		£
Budgeted	80	×	5000 litres per cow	×	17.2p per litre	=	68,800
Actual	75	×	4500 litres per cow	×	16.9p per litre	=	57,000*
Difference	−5		−500 litres per cow		−0.3 per litre		11,800

*Figures have been rounded

(in this case, cows), (b) the yield per unit (i.e. milk per cow) and (c) the price received for each unit of milk. Similar breakdowns will be possible on the cost side of the farm economy, e.g. labour (see Table 6.3).

Arithmetic of this kind is not difficult and has the merit of identifying very clearly where discrepancies lie, and of quantifying them. It helps managers to identify these discrepancies which, when the underlying technical or economic reasons for them are known. can be most easily rectified, as well as identifying those which are the most significant in terms of lost net revenue.

Table 6.3. Comparison of budget and actual performance for labour costs.

	Staff		Wage per employee (£)		£
Budgeted	2	×	10,750	=	21,500
Actual	2	×	11,250	=	22,500
Difference	—		+500		+1,000

For many readers this might, in these days of computers, be too blunt an approach – and we readily agree that something more frequent and more detailed may sometimes be necessary. This might take the form, for example, of a monthly or quarterly cash flow statement (also comparing expectations with actual achievements) or short-term enterprise or input checks which we will consider shortly. A specimen quarterly cash flow based on the whole farm situation shown above, in which actual transactions, in and out, are coupled with measurements of differences, as indicated by the example of milk receipts in the 1st quarter, is shown in Table 6.4.

It will be relatively easy for those with computers, or with computer services, to be furnished regularly with this kind of information, provided a budget has been prepared in the first instance. Computers may even help here, but hand methods will often still suffice. In either case reliable records of past physical performance, preferably relating to several years rather than one, are in our view likely to be the best available guide to what will happen in the near future. On what grounds should we reasonably assume otherwise? Past records are not the useless data some would have us believe – especially when linked to informed guesstimates about current and future prices. We should, however, sound a warning here to the cash flow enthusiasts that a substantial amount of time can be wasted in trying to reconcile differences between planned and actual financial amounts in particular time periods which have been caused simply through accidents of timing of payments and receipts.

SHORT PERIOD ENTERPRISE CHECKS

We have already acknowledged that enterprise control checks are valuable both in their own right and because they offer a more detailed exploration of possible problems that are part and parcel of the whole farm situation. It is, of course, important that errors should be detected and corrected, if at all possible, while they are happening and not at the end of some artificial accounting period.

As a general proposition it would be difficult to disagree with this view,

Table 6.4. A quarterly cash flow sheet.

Item	(Year's Budget)	1st quarter Budgeted	Actual	Difference	2nd quarter Budgeted	Actual	Difference	3rd quarter Budgeted	Actual	Difference	4th quarter Budgeted	Actual	Difference
Receipts													
Crops	(64,000)	17,000	16,500	−500 etc.	12,000			32,000			32,000		
Milk	(68,800)				5,000			21,800			18,000		
Cattle	(15,000)							10,000					
Sub-Total	(147,800)	17,000	16,500	−500 etc.	17,000			63,800			50,000		
Expenditure													
Livestock Purchased	(10,000)				10,000								
Food	(16,800)	2,000			2,000			6,400			6,400		
Seed	(5,500)							2,750			2,750		
Fertilizer	(13,800)	4,600						4,600			4,600		
Rent	(18,600)				9,300						9,300		
Power* and Machinery	(27,600)	6,900			6,900			6,900			6,900		
Labour*	(21,500)	5,375			5,375			5,375			5,375		
Sundries	(16,000)	4,000			4,000			4,000			4,000		
Sub-Total	(129,800)	22,875			37,575			30,025			39,325		
Balance	(18,000)	−5,875			−20,575			+33,775			+10,675		
Cumulative Balance	(18,000)	−5,875**			−26,450			+7,325			+18,000		

*For simplicity it has been assumed that these items are incurred equally in each of the quarters and that the depreciation element of machinery costs is similarly incurred, although in practice it will be represented by periodic caital expenditure.
**If zero from previous period.

but it should be said that there are numerous aspects of farming, including much arable farming and some livestock rearing (as well as in the use of some resources), where little or no corrective action can be applied except when strategic planning and decision-making is under way for the next production cycle. But there are, of course, those enterprises such as dairying, pigs and poultry which do lend themselves to, and do require, short period control checks. In the livestock enterprises mentioned above, food is being dispensed daily, by staff, in order that it may be converted into livestock produce: milk, young pigs or pigmeat and eggs. Efficient food conversion, in these circumstances, is vital and is to a considerable extent in the hands of those carrying out the operation. Careful records are required of the amount of food being used in any time period, its cost, and the amount and value of the produce being generated by this process. We believe that it is important, in order to simplify the control process, to concentrate the recording process of those four items – the ones that determine the vital input:output ratio – and to disregard most other measurements. An increasingly large number of enterprise costing or control schemes are available to farmers sponsored by various organizations in the ancillary sector and we are concerned that some of these are inclined to over-complicate the issues involved; perhaps because they are designed to provide information for the sponsors as well as for the farmer himself; perhaps, also, because of the existence of computers. There is need for discrimination in these areas.

Fig. 6.1. The elements of food conversion.

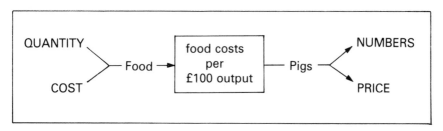

Taking pig fattening as an example, Fig. 6.1 indicates the four crucial elements which determine the measure of food conversion: food fed, food price, pigs sold and pig prices. For 'pigs' we could substitute either eggs or milk.

It is of course possible to go behind those four figures with a more detailed analysis. In our pig example, for instance, the following comparisons may help us to understand in more detail what is happening to pig numbers if that appears to be a problem.

	Budget	*Actual*
Sows farrowed	85	80
Gilts farrowed	15	10
Pigs reared per sow	10	9
Pigs reared per gilt	8	7
Total pigs reared	970	790

Eventually, however, the analysis will run out; husbandry and economic explanations will emerge and then, where it is possible, action on the part of management will hopefully lead to control.

SHORT PERIOD INPUT CHECKS

Turning now to inputs, we differentiate between those which flow continually, like a stream, and those which are controlled like water from a tap. Labour, fuel and feedingstuffs are all of the 'stream' type of expenditure and some form of regular check (possibly a histogram like the one shown in Fig. 6.2) seems desirable, just in case the stream turns into a flood! The payment of rent on the other hand, and the purchase of items like seeds, fertilizers and sprays are more akin to the 'tap' situation. The tap is briefly turned on and then turned off, and when it is off no further control is required. This distinction between stream and tap types of expenditure cuts across the division of costs into the fixed and the variable – another valuable division in terms of decision-making. The one used here is, we believe, just as valuable in terms of control.

INABILITY TO CONTROL

Finally, in considering the application of control methods to farming it must be admitted that there will be many factors influencing both farming operations themselves and the financial outcome of those operations which will be quite outside the control of any manager. The list of those influences hardly needs reproducing. It will make familiar reading to those in the industry. The weather, disease, world market forces, government and international agricultural and economic policies; all of these and more will, from time to time, exert their unexpected influences, but not always in a way which is detrimental to all farmers, and certainly not exclusively towards farmers. Budgetary control is not really about these influences. It is about identifying what has not gone according to plan, measuring the extent of that occurrence, discovering why it happened, identifying the

Fig. 6.2. Control of a 'stream' type of expenditure.

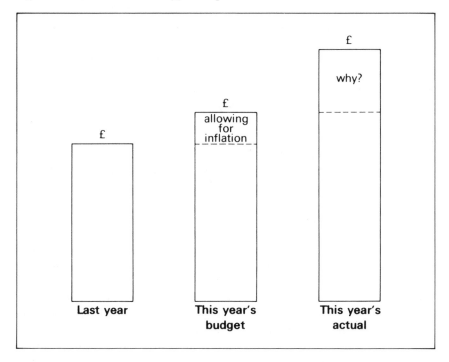

extent to which management can or cannot bring about a correction, and then, where it can, bringing it about. The fact that some of the reasons for failure to achieve a desired result are outside the control of management is neither here nor there. It is certainly not an argument to be used against the application of control methods in farming. On the contrary, we would argue that the more influences at work that are outside the control of management, the more important it becomes to identify items that can be controlled and for careful control then to be exercised. The existence of influences outside the control of management could, therefore, call for a greater application of budgetary control rather than less. The political and economic prospects facing the farming industry as we write suggest to us that more rather than less will be beyond the control of farm businesses as they move into the 1990s.

CONTROL AT THE HEART OF MATTERS

We have tried to demonstrate in this chapter the importance of control and some particular features of its applications in a farming business. Perhaps more than any other topic in this book it comes close to the heart of farming itself. But it also comes close to the heart of effective management and in this sense draws closely together the two disciplines with which this book is concerned: farming and management. We felt it to be important, therefore, that the chapter should close with a few general comments to emphasize the significance of control in this cohesive role. Several points need to be stressed.

First, as we have already said, budgetary control is not just about arithmetic. The arithmetic that is involved can and should be simple. It should enlighten, not confuse. Its main purpose is to direct managers to where corrective action is required. Without that corrective action, no control will have been exercised. With it, effective farming practice and effective management through control will have been combined in an attempt to produce required results. Where this is brought about with the co-operation and contribution of employees, budgetary control will have had a particularly important bonding effect.

Secondly, budgetary control offers the most relevant and pertinent way in which farmers and managers can assess the overall financial results from their business in any particular year. It enables them to judge their results against a tailor-made statement of what they consider to be possible, on their farm, under their management, during the precise twelve months in question. It is a substantially sharper tool than 'comparative analysis' which involves the comparison of results on one farm with standards of performance based on the average or above average results for a group of farms. That is not to suggest that comparative analysis is not useful; it will be discussed in our financial chapter. But most farmers appreciate that no two situations are the same, and whilst the league table spirit is understandable it clearly has its limitations.

It is because of these limitations that we urge farmers towards a budgetary assessment of their results, in addition to, if not as a complete substitute for, comparative analysis. That means that a detailed budget for each ensuing year should be part of every farmer's managerial equipment – although this is still far from being the case.

Thirdly – and this brings us back to the importance of farming techniques and husbandry – there is often more scope for achieving increased profits by improving the level of performance of what is currently being done than by searching for radically different systems of farming. Our observation tells us that the majority of farm systems are reasonably well suited to the resources – including the managers – that are available. If that were not the case it would imply that farmers are bad judges of what is right for them and their farms. Earlier reference, however, to the very wide performance gap which is known to exist in the industry would tend to confirm our contention about the scope for tightening up on technical performance and economic organization within existing enterprises; and that is precisely what budgetary control and supervisory control are concerned with. For the record, we should add that we are not suggesting that nobody should try to do anything new. Sometimes, of course, it will be necessary. But we are saying, think carefully before you do so – especially in the uncharted waters of diversification – and, first, look critically at what you already have and at the possibility for improving it.

Finally we draw attention to the common thought that underlies budgetary control – the attempt to do what you intend to do as well as you can – and the concept of key results areas discussed in our chapter on objectives. Again, from our observation, on many farms there are only a few (sometimes only one) important aspects of management, such as yields on the arable farm; margin over concentrates per forage hectare on the dairy farm; and food costs per £100 output on the pig farm, which really matter, and to which unlimited care and effort should be applied. That thought underlies MBO and it also underlies the concept and techniques of control. It is a theme to which we shall return in our penultimate chapter on priorities.

OUR FINAL THOUGHT

Effective control requires measurement, and when necessary and possible, corrective action; without this action there is no control. There is probably more scope for increasing profits on most farms by a more careful control of the existing system than from radically changing it.

QUESTIONS AND EXERCISES

- What is your reaction to these statements?
  - Control is largely a physical matter
  - Control is an office job
  - Control is the most continual of all management tasks
  - The existence of factors outside the manager's control calls for more control by him, not less.

- Consider:
  - how far you involve your staff in helping you to control each of your principal enterprises
  - the extent to which, in each case, you could increase or improve their role in this respect.

- Identify those of your enterprises which lend themselves to short period control techniques, and in each case:
  - consider the extent to which your existing techniques give you no more and no less than you need
  - identify what you need if it does not already exist.

- Set up an ongoing check on any one of your stream-type expenses, which you feel may not be under strict control.

- If you do not already have them, devote time to preparing:
  - a whole farm budget
  - a projected cash flow
  to be used for control purposes. (See Finance chapter for guidance on these techniques.)

GUIDE TO FURTHER READING

Barnard, C. S. and Nix, J. S. (1979) *Farm Planning and Control.* Cambridge University Press, Cambridge.
  The word 'control' features in the title of this book and the whole of Part IV is devoted to it.

Budgetary Control in Farm Management (1975) Bulletin No. 10, North of Scotland College of Agriculture.
  Provides some useful examples.

Giles, A. K. (1964) *Budgetary Control as an aid to Farm Management.* Miscellaneous Study No. 33. Dept. of Agricultural Economics and Management, University of Reading.
  Remains a standard text on the philosophy and practice of budgetary control.

Rehman, T. (ed.) (1988) *Cutting and Controlling Costs.* Study No. **17**, Farm Management Unit, University of Reading.
  A series of articles providing practical advice.

Sizer, J. (1969) *An Insight into Management Accounting.* Penguin Books, Middlesex.
  Chapter 7 (Budgetary control) is a helpful chapter in a generally helpful book.

Otherwise, this important subject, although underlying much of what is written in the standard texts, tends not to be given the specific attention we believe it deserves. The reader is advised to consult the Subject Index of the CMA Journal *Farm Management* (Vol. **7**, No. **1**, Spring 1989) for reference to particular articles that have appeared on this subject.

PART III

What has to be Managed?

Chapter 7

Production

The concept of production
Building a production plan
Gross margins
Adjusting the plan
Acquiring the resources
Operating the plan

THE CONCEPT OF PRODUCTION

The concept of production is an elusive one. In some respects it is straight-forward enough; it is after all, what much of farming is about – the creation of commodities that, either directly or indirectly, will be turned into food or drink for human consumption. Even these days, when providing services as opposed to creating commodities is a main activity, a production process (in the economic sense) is still involved. The moment, however, one begins to reflect on precisely what is involved (on how production is actually brought about) then the subject becomes more complex.

There are reasons for this complexity. Production is the co-ordinating process which brings together capital and labour in its various forms – raw materials, processed goods and equipment of all kinds, plant, technology, the workforce and management – in order to create the commodity or, increasingly in agriculture, as it looks for new markets and opportunities, the service that is required. It is, however, difficult for us to visualize production in the way that we can identify factors of production such as land or a piece of machinery, or even some of the managerial functions that have been discussed in earlier chapters. In farming, we cannot always see production while it is happening and sometimes we cannot even measure it, at least until the end of a production cycle.

In these circumstances we may be tempted to turn to the literature of farming and farm management in order to find a proper perspective on the subject, but here again we may be frustrated. Production so often means different things to different people. The subject is so all-embracing and can be approached from so many different specialized standpoints that overall views are easily lost. We may, for example, read about farming systems, about labour organization, about technology and husbandry or about the application of operational research techniques to farming. Each of these subjects may purport to be about production and yet we may still be left with the feeling that the real essence of production has not been fully explained to us.

In this situation it may be tempting to conclude that there is no such thing as a separate production process; that it is merely the result of the co-ordination of various other processes which require specialized resources and skills. But that view, of course, denies the all-important contribution from management in co-ordinating inputs and transforming them into outputs. Far from denying the existence of production as a process, we are of the view that it is one of the central responsibilities of management. As suggested earlier, it is at the very heart of farming itself and it is not surprising that continuing financial success in a farming business will often, in the last resort, depend upon the ability of the manager to organize an effective production system.

We see three essential ingredients to the process of transforming inputs into output:

---

1. Building a production plan, having due regard to market opportunities, available fixed resources, and the facility for adjustment.
2. Acquiring the necessary resources and employing them in the appropriate combination.
3. Operating the plan, with due regard to required levels of performance and appropriate supervision.

Each of these three topics will be discussed more fully in the remainder of this chapter but before that we will digress, briefly, in order to discuss one or two economic concepts which are relevant.

First is the concept of effective demand. It was hinted at in our definition of management in Chapter 2, when we referred to the production of a commodity or service which is both wanted and can be offered at a price that will be paid. This concept underlies much of what follows in this chapter. In economic terms demand always means effective demand. It implies that the desire to buy something on the part of an individual or a group of individuals is backed by an ability and willingness to buy at a given price.

Hardly surprisingly this concept has vital implications for the producer, and never has the farming community had to be more aware of the effective demand of its consumers than at the present – an awareness that will no doubt become more important as 1992 arrives and passes. Under normal competitive conditions, where market prices are determined for rather than by them (as it is for farmers) producers will need to produce at a level of economic efficiency which, at the reigning prices of the commodities they are selling, will yield an acceptable profit. if that is not the case, then sooner or later they will be out of business. At any given set of prices and costs he will be concerned with economic efficiency rather than with technical efficiency that ignores effective demand. As a matter of fact we have never been quite sure how to define the term 'technical efficiency'. If it implies some notion of a technically perfect animal or crop, produced without blemish and with the highest quality materials and care, but for which there is no effective demand, then it is not a very helpful concept to the farmer who wishes to remain in business. This is not, of course, to deny the merits of doing things well within the limits of existing prices and costs. We have already noted that it is the final litres of milk and tonnes of grain which add to profit. It often costs as much to do things badly as to do them well, so that doing things well in this productive sense is usually in harmony with economic efficiency; and even if farmers and farm managers are not always interested in literally maximizing profits – and these days may temper their desire for profits with a concern for green issues – at the end of the day they simply cannot ignore the need for economic efficiency. On the contrary they will often twist and turn in reaching their decisions about what to produce, what methods to use, and how much to produce in an endeavour to generate profits which are acceptable to them in their particular circumstances.

Economists deal with these three questions – what to produce, by what methods to produce and how much to produce – in their so-called 'theory of the firm'. It describes those conditions which have to exist if profits are to be maximized. It is not necessary for practising farmers to have a detailed knowledge of this theory, but to the extent that it underlies some of the principles and tools that are used in elementary farm planning, a brief word about it is appropriate.

The question of what to produce is referred to in economists' jargon as a product-product type of question. It relates to the combination of one enterprise with another, or with others. Equilibrium will be reached (i.e. the point where there is no further incentive to change the combination) when, at any given set of prices and costs, equal returns are being received from the last unit of resources employed in each enterprise. Equi-marginal returns are then said to exist. If greater returns accrue from the marginal use of resources in one enterprise as opposed to another, then a further direction of resources to that enterprise would be indicated. To take a simple example, if a choice lies between two enterprises, A and B, each using scarce resource X, and if the return from the use of each extra unit of X is greater if devoted to enterprise A than to B (situation 1), then it is sensible to concentrate the use of resources in enterprise A until such time as there is no difference between the return to A and to B. At that point equi-marginal returns are said to exist, and at least so far as choice between A and B is concerned, the system is in equilibrium (situation 2).

	Enterprise	
	A	B
Value of marginal unit of X	1	1
1. Value of marginal returns from unit of X	3	2
2. Value of marginal returns from unit of X when equi-marginal returns exist	2	2

The question of what methods to employ within an enterprise (i.e. how much machinery, how much labour, and so on) is known as a factor-factor question. It has that name because it is concerned with the combination of factors of production, rather than with the combination of enterprises, and equilibrium is reached when the last unit of capital spent on one factor of production yields the same return as the last unit spent on any other. If this were not the case a redirection of capital in favour of one factor at the expense of another would be called for – fertilizer on grass instead of concentrated food, for example.

To illustrate this point with simple figures again, with two inputs, A and B, being employed in any particular enterprise, the advantage initially lies in the continued use of A as against B (with the marginal return to A being twice that of B i.e. situation 1) until such time as, with diminishing returns, the two are equal; equi-marginal returns then exist between the use of A and B and equilibrium is reached (situation 2).

	Resource	
	A	B
Value of marginal unit used	1	1
1. Value of return to marginal unit used	4	2
2. Value of marginal return to marginal unit used when equi-marginal returns exist	2	2

Thirdly, the question of how much to produce, is known as a factor-product question, in which equilibrium is reached when the last unit of capital spent in any direction (the marginal cost) equals the additional receipts generated (the marginal revenue), i.e. situation B below.

	Situation		
	A	B	C
Revenue from marginal unit of production	2	2	2
Cost of marginal unit of production	1	2	3

To stop short of this point (i.e. situation A, when marginal costs are still below the marginal revenue) would be to ignore some remaining opportunities of gain, however small. To go beyond it (i.e. situation C, when costs become greater than receipts) would be to begin to reduce profits or incur losses. This is an important concept when considering the scale of activities as opposed to the two previous questions that were concerned with balance of enterprises and pattern of inputs.

Overall equilibrium will only have been reached when there is no incentive to change in any of the three directions that we have discussed, i.e. in the combination of enterprises, in the methods of production and in the overall scale of production.

BUILDING A PRODUCTION PLAN

That was perhaps a rather long excursion into economic thinking, stemming from the mention of effective demand, technical efficiency and economic efficiency, but we believe it to be important. We can now revert to the more familiar farming scene. It will have been clear to the reader that very few farmers need to think precisely in the ways that have just been outlined. All kinds of practical considerations prohibit this. There is, for instance, the simple fact (already noted) that most of them do not necessarily aim to maximize profits; the fact that very often, because of the complications of costs that are shared between enterprises, farmers will not know, in detail, the marginal costs associated with each of their enterprises, the problem that extra inputs of lumpy resources like labour and machinery, for example, cannot be employed in small incremental units; and the existence of such personal feelings as caution, not wanting to farm to the brink, and having regard for the long-term consequences of farming decisions as well as the short-term ones. Nevertheless, it is our experience that farmers are, in their own way, familiar with the kind of questions that were posed in the preceding paragraphs. They will, for example, consider carefully the allocation of land, labour and capital between the different enterprises on their farms; they will also explore ways and means (taking due notice of research and development work) of producing in a least-cost way; and they will have to make decisions about the scale and intensity of their businesses – recognizing, for instance, when increasing returns seem likely to give way to diminishing returns, and the opportunities for profitable expansion run out.

Notwithstanding the constraints that inhibit them from applying economic theory in practice, farmers and their advisers do find it useful to pick out the pieces of theory that help. A good example of this is the general recognition that is given by the farming community to the distinction between fixed and variable cost – a distinction which is at the heart of the gross margin concept, so commonly used in farm planning and which we shall consider shortly. It is therefore against this mixed background of theory and practice that we can turn more directly to the question of building a production plan and consider three broadly different approaches to the task, distinguished from each other by their degree of sophistication.

First, there are methods based on simple subjective decisions made by farmers on the basis of the resources at their disposal, of what has been happening previously, and of their personal experience and inclinations. This is not a sophisticated approach but it should not be criticized for that. It may be especially appropriate where there is little or no choice of activity and where the farmer's own judgement is proven. It is also important to remember that when an individual is doing what he wants to do he is likely to produce the best results anyhow. A system of farming embarked upon in this way can be evaluated by orthodox budgeting in which the physical elements of the plan (i.e. the number of livestock, acres of crops, and resources needed) will be priced in order to arrive at the predicted profit. Taking the same example that was used in the previous chapter of a farmer on, say, a 150 hectare lowland farm, suitable for good quality grassland and arable farming, he or she might simply decide to divide the farm between two historically reliable cornerstones of (UK) farming – dairy cows and cereals. The size of the dairy herd (80 cows) originally determined perhaps by a number that can be conveniently handled by one man (and more recently, perhaps, by quota) might require say, 40 hectares with the balance of the farm (110 hectares) in cereals. Two staff are to be employed (a cowherd and tractor driver) and the budget for the farm's income potential (at the time of writing) might be as shown in Table 7.1.

There are many farms where the production plans have originated and evolved in this way. Many such farms are known to us personally and we do not denigrate the approach. It relies on experience, judgement, and intuition – valuable attributes in any manager.

Our second broad approach to building a production programme

Table 7.1. Budget for a dairy and cereals farm.

Gross output	£	Total £
Crops		
65 ha winter wheat (6.9 t/ha) @ £98/t	43,953	
45 ha spring barley (4.7 t/ha) @ £94/t	19,881	63,834
Milk		
80 cows (5,000 litre/cow) @ 17.2p/litre		68,800
Cattle		
15 cull cows @ £400 each	6,000	
75 calves @ £120 each	9,000	15,000
Total		147,634

Expenses	£	Total £
Livestock		
15 heifers @ £650 each		9,750
Purchased feed		
80 cows (1.4t) @ £150/t		16,800
Seed		
65 ha winter wheat @ £42/ha	2,730	
45 ha spring barley @ £42/ha	1,890	
10 ha grass @ £75/ha	750	5,370
Fertilizers		
65 ha winter wheat @ £90/ha	5,850	
45 ha spring barley @ £70/ha	3,150	
40 ha grass @ £120/ha	4,800	13,800
Other costs		
Rent and rates @ £124/ha	18,600	
Power and machinery @ £184/ha	27,600	
Paid labour (2 people)	21,554	
Sundries @ £100/ha	15,000	82,754
Net farm income		19,160
Total		147,634

encompasses all those methods which, while hand operated (as opposed to those that are computerized), rely on much more objective and systematic assessment and selection than our first method. These more systematic methods have in common that they employ the gross margin concept in one form or another. At the most elementary level, gross margins are calculated and then enterprises are selected in descending order of gross margin per unit.

GROSS MARGINS

We should pause at this point to say something about the gross margin concept itself. It has a variety of uses in farm business planning and analysis and, although this has not always been the case, it now has widespread acceptance amongst farmers, consultants and teachers alike. Contrary to popular belief, its origins can be traced well back beyond the years of its popularization. Indeed, it first made its appearance in Reading University as far back as the early 1920s and, some years later, appeared again in the publication of farm income data in Northern Ireland. Its first major use as a management tool in England, however, was in the Eastern Counties in the early 1960s, when David Wallace of Cambridge University recognized its value in a farming locality where the choice of enterprises was of paramount importance. It does not, as we have already said, measure profit. It is an inappropriate measure, for instance, in price-fixing discussions when, understandably, farmers will wish *all* costs – not just the variable ones – to be taken into account. When, however, a farming system and modifications to it are being considered, that is not necessarily the case. Fixed costs often do remain fixed in the face of minor modifications to a system, and in those circumstances it is the effect of variations in output and variable costs which need to be explored. This does not mean that fixed costs will never alter in magnitude, even in the short term – inflation alone will see to that. But it does mean that various enterprise combinations may be possible, and that small alterations to a system will be possible, without necessarily altering the level of fixed costs. The fact that the so-called fixed costs (regular labour, machinery, rent and overheads) are likely to vary considerably in magnitude from farm to farm, and that the variable costs (materials and casual labour) often do not, is an irrelevance.

Table 7.2 shows examples (again using rounded figures) of gross margin calculations for four very different types of enterprise: cereals, cash roots, grazing livestock and intensive livestock. These examples are shown here more to demonstrate the method of calculating gross margin than to suggest that the calculations typify any particular situation or represent any sort of norm; certainly none of them is likely to remain constant for any length of time and the reader would be advised to remember that they have

Table 7.2. Gross margin calculations for cereals, cash roots, grazing livestock and intensive factory livestock enterprises.

1. Cereals

	Winter wheat		Spring barley	
Gross Output	6.9 t @ £98/t	**676**	4.7t @ £94/t	**442**
Variable Costs				
seed	180 kg @ 23p/kg	42	175 kg @ 24p/kg	42
fertilizers	155N, 50P, 50K	90	150N, 55P, 55K	70
sprays		86		36
Total variable costs		**218**		**148**
Gross Margin		**458**		**294**

2. Cash root crops

	Potatoes (main crop)		Sugar beet	
Gross Output	32 t @ £90/t	**2880**	38 t @ £30/t	**1140**
Variable Costs				
seed	2.7 t @ £138/t	373	6 kg @ 13p/kg	79
fertilizers	220N, 275P, 275K	200	110N, 65P, 190K (incl. salt)	125
spray		138		123
casual labour		170		
transport				150
sundries (bags, PMB levy etc)		350		15
Total variable costs		**1231**		**492**
Gross Margin		**1649**		**648**

Table 7.2 continued.

3. Grazing livestock (£/ha)

	Dairy cows (Friesian)		Lowland beef single sucking autumn calving		Beef – Autumn born calves (18 month fattening)		Sheep (fat lamb production)	
Gross Output	5000 l @ 17.2p/l	860	Weaned calf @ 6–9 mths	420	480 kg live-weight @ £1.16/kg	557	1.5 lambs	56
	Value of calf	120	Suckler cow subsidy	47			Ewe premium	6
							Wool	4
		980		**467**				**66**
(Less)	Cow depreciation	−40	Cow and bull depreciation	−42	Calf purchase	−199	Ewe depreciation	−15
		940		**425**		**358**		**51**
Variable Costs/unit								
concentrate	1.4 t	210	0.4 t	56	1.3 t	156	55 kg	8
sundries		75		22		45		8
forage crop	0.5 forage ha/cow	75	0.6 forage ha/cow	60	0.3 forage ha/head	38	9 ewes/forage ha	8
Total variable costs		360		138		239		24
Gross Margin/unit		580		287		119		27
Gross Margin/ha		1160		478		397		243

4. Intensive enterprises (£/unit)

	Breeding sows		Bacon pigs		Hens (100 laying-birds)		Intensive beef	
Gross Output	22.5 weaners @ £30 each	675	68 kg dead-weight @ 1.40/kg	95	2200 doz. eggs @ 50p/doz.	1110	446 kg live-weight @ £1.18/kg	526
(Less)	sow depreciation	−20	weaner cost	−30	repl. cost	−192	cost of calf	−195
		655		**65**		**908**		**331**
Variable Costs								
concentrates	2.0 t	320	0.25 t	36	4.9 t	700	1.8 t	225
sundries		50		4		65		16
Total variable costs		**370**		**40**		**765**		**241**
Gross Margin		**285**		**25**		**143**		**90**

been made in the UK in the early 1990s.

It will be abundantly clear from these examples that the gross margin does not measure profit, but rather the contribution that an enterprise can make towards covering the fixed costs of a farming system and then providing a profit.

Perhaps, therefore, the greatest asset of the gross margin is the fact that it measures, in one composite figure, the effect of the physical efficiency with which an individual converts certain variable inputs (with the help of other more fixed inputs) into a saleable product. It is thus a valuable indicator of efficiency within an enterprise on any particular farm. It should be remembered, however, that different farms may well use resources in different combinations (for instance, more regular labour – a fixed cost; and less casual labour – a variable cost) so that inter-farm comparisons of gross margins can be dangerous. Equally dangerous is the assumption that when small changes occur on a particular farm, changes in profitability can always be measured simply by manipulating gross margins. The possibility of lumpy changes in the fixed costs must always be looked for. How and when they occur will depend on the situation on the farm in question. Two farms making identical farming changes may well be 'jumping off' from different points and the effect of the change on the fixed costs may be quite different in the two circumstances. That is why the use of the partial budget (discussed in Chapter 9) which looks at every item of cost and return that undergoes change, is often what is required. Gross margins can be part of that process. Sometimes they will suffice by themselves but sometimes they will not, depending upon the scale and type of change that is involved. It should never, therefore, be assumed that gross margins are totally adequate by themselves, and no farmer or adviser who understands the data he is handling will be in danger of making that assumption.

We can now conclude our discussion of gross margins as such and return to the business of building a production plan. Before doing so, however, we would like to mention two more points.

First, to the extent that, in Europe at least, there is also a frequent tendency to present global financial results for different farming systems in the gross margin and fixed cost form, and that gross margins are now being used as a basis for measuring farm size and type, we may reasonably expect to find this measure in increased rather than reduced use in the years ahead. Anyone in the UK looking for examples of gross margins for different enterprises, with an indication of all the variables that they can embrace, can do no better than to refer to an up-to-date issue of the *Farm Management Pocketbook*, prepared annually by John Nix at Wye College.

Secondly, we have detected in recent years, alongside the use of gross margins, a renewed desire on the part of some farmers to have recourse to more fully costed statements of enterprise results – the net margin as it is called. We sympathize with that view and will comment on it in our financial chapter.

BUILDING A PRODUCTION PLAN – CONTINUED

It will be recalled that our second broad approach to building a production plan incorporated those methods in which, one way or another, the gross margin per unit of the scarcest resource (often but not necessarily land) is used as a basis for assessing and selecting enterprises into the system. Used in its elementary way the gross margin approach to planning may provide only a slight advance on the subjective method just discussed. At the other end of the gross margin scale, however, it may be used, still in a hand-operated way, to select a production system which takes full account of the available resources, the possible enterprises and the constraints operating on both. Such methods are known collectively as 'programme planning'. There are numerous variations on this theme, and it is unlikely to matter much which particular version is used. What is more important here, is that some approach is used, at least where the planning problem is sufficiently complex to warrant it, which has a degree of objectivity as is reasonably systematic – minimizing the risk of wrong decisions. This approach, then, involves something like the following step by step approach:

1. A detailed consideration of the resources that are available – land, labour and capital – with special recognition of whichever is most scarce.

2. A review of the available marketing opportunities and requirements – with a special regard for effective demand.

3. A consideration, in the light of (1.) and (2.) and of personal preferences, of all of the enterprises that could comprise the production programme – not necessarily just the existing ones.

4. The calculation of the 'normalized' gross margins (i.e. taking account of known performance over a number of years and anticipated future costs and prices) for each of the enterprises, using published standard data, appropriately adapted, for new enterprises. The gross margins should be expressed in terms of the unit of the scarcest resource, and more often than not, in this country, it will be land.

5. A consideration of the various physical limits that must be set to the scale of each enterprise, depending upon the existence of such factors as buildings, rotational considerations, seasonal deadlines, quotas and the farmer's own personal preferences.

6. The selection of each enterprise, in descending order of gross margin per unit, to its predetermined limit, continuing until the scarcest resource is exhausted.

7. A check that no other scarce resource has been exhausted. If it has (e.g. labour or capital) explore the possibilities of expanding the supply of that resource, or substituting into the plan, some (or more) of any enterprise that has yet to reach its limit and which will reduce the demands on the resource in question to acceptable levels.

8. The possible introduction of other enterprises making no demands on the scarcest resource, e.g. intensive livestock.

9. The calculation of total gross margin for the final selection of enterprises.

10. The subtraction of fixed costs from total gross margin to determine the profit.

Using the essence of this approach, the situation on the hypothetical 150 hectare dairy and corn farm referred to earlier in this chapter might have been brought about by the following appraisal procedure and methods of enterprise selection. After a detailed consideration of the resources available – with land, as it often is, as the scarcest (step 1) and a review of the market opportunities which present themselves (2) our farmer would decide, taking full account of his or her previous experience and present personal preference, which enterprises to consider in the plan (3). Assuming that he or she decides upon a combination of cows and corn the farmer would then (4) calculate the normalized gross margins which we will assume to correspond to the gross margin example previously shown:

Dairy cows	£1160 per hectare
Wheat	£458 per hectare
Barley	£294 per hectare

Next, in considering the scale of enterprise (5) we will assume that our farmer has set a limit on his cows of 80 (requiring 40 hectares) and that the remainder of the farm (110) can be in cereals, but that for some reason only 65 hectares can be in wheat. Enterprises are then selected (6) in descending order of gross margins per hectare, each to its predetermined limit, until the scarcest resource (land) is exhausted, resulting in the following farm system:-

Dairy cows	40 ha @ £1160 GM/ha	= 46,400
Wheat	65 ha @ £458 GM/ha	= 29,770
Barley	45 ha @ £294 GM/ha	= 13,230

Total gross margin (GM)   89,400

It now remains (7) for the farmer to check that the limits of the availability of other resources (e.g. labour, capital) have not been exceeded – and to make any adjustments to the system (possibly even including the substitution of a hitherto unconsidered enterprise (8)) that will ease the resource situation and enable the system to function. In some versions of Programme Planning this process of substituting one activity for another can itself become very sophisticated. Examples of this can be found in *Farm Planning and Control* (Barnard and Nix). We have confined our illustration here to the less complex approach often referred to simply as 'ordered budgeting' which we believe to be appropriate for the readership we are addressing.

When (9) the total gross margin has been calculated (£89,400), the final step (10) is for the fixed costs (in this case estimated to be £70,240) to be subtracted from the gross margin in order to arrive at the potential profit from the system in the year in question (£19,160).

The third basic approach to building a farm plan is where, because of the complexity of the available choices between enterprises and the range of resource constraints, recourse is made to a computer. Several computerized planning methods are in existence, the most well known of them involving linear programming. There has been plenty of evidence that such techniques are a helpful aid to advisers and consultants in arriving at modal farm plans that can be adapted to individual circumstances. There is, however, despite a lot of development work by various advisory agencies, little evidence to suggest that these kinds of approach are being widely used on individual farms, and we do not envisage the situation changing substantially. Such techniques usually require an experienced adviser, backed by computer resources and personnel that increasingly will have to be paid for by the client, and, despite the speed with which profit-maximizing solutions can be generated once problems have been properly formulated, the overall time involved will usually have to concede something to more 'back of the envelope' methods – just as those methods will have to concede something to computer methods in their objectivity, accuracy and depth. It is the intention of this book to concentrate on those procedures that practising farmers and farm managers are likely to use and so we do not propose to illustrate computerized planning techniques – but refer the interested reader to the appropriate references at the end of the chapter. The special edition of the CMA's Journal *Farm Management*, summarizing a wide range of planning techniques, remains, although published in 1969, a valuable guide.

Our considered reflection on these three different approaches to farm planning is that while traditional budgeting based on subjective decisions may still suffice in many cases, the time has long since arrived when, certainly in the more complex farming situations, something more systematic and objective should be preferred. But at the same time, despite the increasing use of computers on farms, there is a very large number of farms where the basic planning problem is insufficiently complicated to warrant computerized methods.

This reasoning leads us to the conclusion that some variant of the second approach – 'ordered budgeting' – is probably the most appropriate planning tool on many farms. In our preference for this 'middle way' we are aware that it lacks both the ease of the more subjective approach and the precision of the more objective ones; that the arithmetic can, in fact, become complicated and that the method falls between two stools. We accept that there is some force in these arguments, but we argue that unless the process is made complicated by the user, the arithmetic can be kept simple; that the result will be based upon more rigorous and methodical thinking than the *ad hoc* approach of subjective budgeting; and that – an important point – the method (unlike computerized ones) can be applied by any of the farmers and farm managers to whom this book is addressed.

It is, of course, common to all methods of farm planning that any chosen programme relates to a given set of fixed resources. If those resources are altered, the situation calls for a reselection of the enterprises that would be feasible in those changed circumstances. Net margins may be a more important concept here than gross margins.

ADJUSTING THE PLAN

Important though devising the plan in the first place may be, it is not something that has to be done too often; once a year at the most and perhaps less often than that. It will, however, be essential to keep a critical eye on the almost inevitable need to adjust the plan from time to time, if only to meet the consequences of constantly changing prices and costs.

A systematic approach to this rather nagging aspect of farm planning can be as helpful as it is in devising an overall plan in the first place. In this context we have found it helpful to explore the opportunities for profit-improving adjustments within the framework of the following four different kinds of change:

---

1. Improving gross margins within existing enterprises, whether as a result of physical input : output improvements, marketing improvements or in the purchase and use of variable costs. The possibilities here are endless. They are at the very heart of production and do not necessarily mean more physical production.

2. Altering the system of farming, by substitutions at the margin, in favour of enterprises yielding the higher gross margins. This could include the introduction of entirely new enterprises and, coupled with possible reductions in fixed costs, changes in the reverse direction, i.e. existing enterprises making excessive claims or fixed costs being removed from the system. System changes of this kind will encourage a constant re-appraisal of just where realistic limits to enterprises really lie. Changes in economic circumstances have often been known to create changes in thinking about what is and what is not possible.

3. Reducing fixed costs, with or without a change in the pattern of enterprises.

4. Adding to the economic base of the business, by the introduction of fresh land, new enterprises not requiring land, or new non-farming activities. The recent emphasis on diversification and 'value added' activities has made this an increasingly explored option.

Diagrammatically these four possible ways of adding to profit can be represented in the model of a three-enterprise farm presented in Fig. 7.1.

We believe that every possible kind of change can be considered under one or other of these four headings and we encourage periodic and systematic reviews of farm businesses in this way. The time will come when the opportunities to improve under each heading will be exhausted, a fact which should not be overlooked. Improving gross margins, for instance, will require improved management in one form or another and, even where this is possible, that possibility will diminish as each improvement is achieved, unless there are favourable changes in market prices. Diminishing returns are a barrier to the endless intensification of farming methods. Sooner or later, also, husbandry or other practical considerations will call a halt to adjustments to farming systems. Reductions in fixed costs may sometimes be possible especially in the sphere of machinery or labour costs, but it is seldom the case that reductions of this kind can be repeated. Lumpy inputs, like labour and machinery, really are indivisible. Finally, an expansion of the economic base of the business will usually require new capital, possibly some new skills and maybe some degree of luck (as when extra land becomes available in a convenient site and at an acceptable price) and none of these things can be made to order.

Fig. 7.1. Model of a three-enterprise farm.

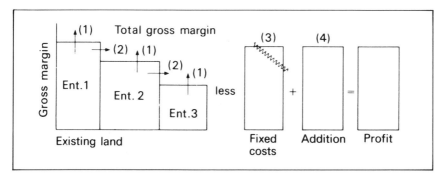

Just in case the last paragraph has a pessimistic sound to it, let it be said that there are no farms that we know where the possibilities under all four headings have run out. Few farmers, even after years of improvement and development, would claim that each enterprise on their farm was being operated at optimum efficiency, with no scope whatever for improvement, and few would feel there was no scope for adjustment in their system. Changing a system slightly can sometimes be the most painless kind of change to make. It does not call for better management, but simply for a different combination of activities. Trying to become better at something may be more difficult, and it is in that area that the advisory services have their part to play. At all events, we urge that every possibility of improving the use of existing resources should be thoroughly explored before new activities, requiring new resources, are introduced. Diversification may be an answer for some; it seems unlikely to be a panacea for all.

ACQUIRING AND EMPLOYING THE REQUIRED RESOURCES

Having developed an optimal plan in terms of utilizing the major resources of land, labour, capital and management ability, the operation of the plan involves the provision of a wide range of additional resources. Here we are right back into practical farming. The required resources include everyday items such as fuel and spare parts, seed, feedingstuffs or replacement breeding stock, as well as the services of specialists such as contractors or veterinarians. The manager needs to know where to obtain these resources, a subject that will be discussed in more detail in our chapter on acquiring information, but has also to consider how much of the resource to buy, the price, quality, timeliness of delivery and the date when payment is due. In addition, it is necessary with many inputs to consider the transport, unloading arrangements and required storage facilities. In practice, it is seldom possible to have the best of all worlds and decisions have to be made to reach a compromise. Take, for instance, a cereal grower purchasing seed for autumn use. Early ordering and delivery widens the choice of variety and grade and enables increased discounts to be obtained, but it may well involve earlier payment. Reception of the consignment ahead of planting time ensures that the seed is on hand for timely drilling, but it involves storage, double-handling or the use of trailers or other vehicles which are not then available for other purposes. In so many situations the chances of producing higher yields of a quality product are increased if the appropriate resources are available at the optimum time. the increased value of output will usually more than cover additional costs leaving an improved margin for the efficient obtainer of resources. It is seen once again that the manager's tasks involves planning, making decisions and, especially, getting priorities right.

The time and effort required by management to obtain resources varies considerably from one type to another. Inputs such as electricity and water flow into the farm as required, with usage easily measured and therefore not difficult to record. Emergency breaks to supply can be overcome by the availability of stand-by generators, staff having ready access to a list of appropriate telephone numbers, and site plans which indicate supply routes and the location of switches or stop valves. Many other farm inputs such as fuel, feedingstuffs and fertilizers are ordered without difficulty according to recognized grades or specifications. Specialized advice may be required before an order can be placed for chemical pesticides or animal medicines, the latter possibly only available on veterinary prescription.

In order to receive delivery of a required input at the appropriate time, several factors have to be taken into account: first, the time lag between placement of the order and expected delivery, secondly, the rate of use, which is often obtained from a recording scheme, and thirdly, the quantity in stock. Having this information readily to hand is an important area of efficient production management. It involves such factors as the neat and tidy stacking of stores, graduated marks on the walls of storage bins and flow meters, and dipsticks or sight-glasses for use with liquids in tanks. As well as enabling quick and accurate stock-taking to take place, such procedures encourage accurate record-keeping. A system for checking deliveries, filing delivery notes and issuing despatch documents is another important aspect of this subject. With the increasing tendency to handle commodities in bulk, there is a justification, especially on the larger holdings, for installing weighing devices so as to be able to monitor the inputs and outputs of production.

The farm staff need to understand their role and authority in obtaining resources. Procedures for calling the vet, ordering fuel or obtaining spare parts need to be discussed, agreed and perhaps committed to paper. Managers may be able to delegate the task of ordering routine inputs but they should at all times be kept in the picture. In larger businesses, routine reports may be prepared with section heads which cover this item, or there may be an arrangement whereby the manager signs official orders to confirm telephone orders by employees.

With the continued trend towards increased mechanization and automation of farms, coupled with the wide range of machines and equipment in use, the supply of spare parts becomes an important part of production management. Reliance on mechanical feeding equipment or manure handling in livestock units means a need for prompt repair of breakdowns, but in arable farming, too, delays to planting, spraying or harvesting operations caused by lack of spares can be costly. Cash flow considerations on the part of dealers and agents often result in minimal stocks of spares being carried locally, so that it is necessary to contact manufacturers direct and arrange long distance transport, or perhaps co-operate in the holding of spares with other local users of identical equipment. Instruction books and spare parts lists need to be readily accessible from files in the office or workshop, ideally with another copy being left with the operator. A very efficient labelling and re-ordering system has been observed on one farm, where each sizeable part in the farm workshop store carries a label bearing the name of the supplier, the model and part number. When a member of staff uses a part, the label is removed and put into a tray, which forms the basis of a shopping list. When the new part arrives, the same label is tied on before it is placed on the shelf. Such a system greatly aids day-to-day management of a busy farm and at the same time demonstrates to staff that management is prepared to provide an efficient back-up service.

Adjustments to a production plan will at times also necessitate the need for additional inputs of a major resource such as land. A successful potato or vegetable grower may develop his market outlets to a stage where production from the existing farm falls short of meeting demand. Disease considerations prevent any shortening of the rotation, so that additional suitable land must be leased from neighbours (potato quota permitting) on an annual basis. Expanding the area of land, if on a temporary basis, also has the advantage of spreading the cost of expensive machinery such as pea viners or combines. A sheep farmer known to us takes land from adjacent cereal growers for a two year ley break in order to expand the size of his flock. He provides seed, fertilizer and fences, removing his stock in time for early ploughing of the second year ley for wheat. Few problems arise, but considerable time was initially involved negotiating the mutually satisfactory arrangement, and especially in calculating the charge. There are obvious attractions in farming additional land, especially to the person who has a long-term objective of increasing the size of the business. The location of additional fields as well as any specific difficulties such as access or the availability of water have a marked effect upon their contribution to the business. Travelling between blocks of land is not only expensive in machinery costs, but it occupies time and makes it more likely that when problems arise, the manager is in the wrong part of the farm. Opportunities to improve the output potential of existing acres should not therefore be overlooked before expanding the size of a farm. Improvements to drainage, lime status and sward quality of permanent pasture by surface treatment can have a marked effect upon the efficiency of forage production.

The need to increase building capacity is common in many farming situations. Legislation in the UK has, for instance, created the need for specialized chemical stores and, for participation in herd health schemes, the requirement for cattle isolation pens.

Technological developments enable additional capital to be justifiably invested, as with facilities to store produce resulting from higher yields or new varieties. In animal production, there is, for example, the justification for specialized flat-deck cages to accommodate piglets weaned at three weeks of age or storage facilities for the components of complete cattle diets. Considerable management input is essential in planning for farm buildings, not only in regard to the financial implications but also to their location, layout, appearance, maintenance and future expansion.

The management of staff is dealt with in a separate chapter, but it is appropriate to mention at this point the many situations in which an additional, if only temporary, input of labour is required. Many intensive fruit and vegetable enterprises, for example, operate with a small permanent staff but depend heavily upon obtaining sufficient casual workers to plant, prune, harvest and grade their crops. The processing of turkeys and capons for the Christmas trade is another example of an enterprise where in order to provide the market with a fresh, high quality product at the optimum time, an additional short-term labour input may be required. The people doing such jobs often return to the same farm each year, and although the work may in some circumstances be rather unpleasant, because it is only for a short period the workers enjoy the change and the extra money. Where skills are required, they are seldom lost from one year to another, but such workers vary widely in the degree of supervision required. Involvement of regular full-time staff with the part-time team needs to be handled with care. Regulars should understand that they are the key workers, and casuals will not be keen to return on future occasions if they feel that they are not appreciated and given all the dirty jobs.

The majority of farms need from time to time to employ specialists who bring into the business skills which are not available in the regular staff, such as the veterinary surgeon, the agronomist and the seed crop inspector. The particular skills may even be available on the farm, as with the shepherd and the job of shearing but, due to pressure of other work, it may in some circumstances be preferable to employ skilled help in order to get the job done more quickly and more efficiently. When contractors are employed not only do they provide equipment, but also (ideally) a skilled operator. The cost of employing such a service may on the face of it appear high, especially if the skills and even the machinery already exist in the business, but the benefits of additional output from improved timeliness should more than cover the cost involved. The contractor who provides efficiently operated machinery is becoming a more important resource to a wide range of farming situations. With the cost of purchasing and maintaining specialized items of equipment continuing to increase, the contractor will find an expanding demand so long as he can provide a reliable service. The need for timeliness cannot be over-emphasized. It is obvious with such operations as combining or hay baling, but the delaying of other jobs, such as hedge trimming or manure handling, can cause loss of potential output if ploughing, cultivations or the yarding of cattle cannot take place at the planned time.

Before leaving the subject of additional labour inputs, the need for relief services, and the part they play, should be mentioned. And the size of the workforce on many farms continues to decline, and as holiday entitlement increases, the need to employ occasional help becomes more frequent. Agencies are in the business to meet such a need but difficulties do arise especially in the area of supervision of the short-term employees. Some producers are overcoming the problem by forming groups so as to employ a regular person who carries out the relief duties for the members. So much for the acquisition of resources.

OPERATING THE PLAN

The third and most important part of production is the operation or implementation of the plan. It is all about getting the job done. It entails the organization of resources – the most appropriate resources – so that they are in the right place at the right time. Once again, it involves many of those aspects of management discussed in the early chapters of this book, i.e. setting targets, planning, decision-making, communicating and controlling, as applicable to the short term. Plans need to be adjusted frequently in order to account for outside influences such as weather conditions, market situations and disease outbreaks.

Production in the majority of farm situations does not mean just one straightforward job; it involves numerous operations which usually need to be carried out in a particular sequence, for example, drilling maize, then rolling, followed by the application of pre-emergence herbicide. The critical job is the one upon which other jobs are dependent, and which therefore has to be given priority. Ploughs need to be kept ahead on heavy land in the autumn, and mowers need to be kept ahead of forage harvesters when wilting is required – otherwise the whole operation comes to a halt if the critical job stops. Sharpening the blades of a precision chop forage harvester should, for instance, take place outside the normal shift so as not to hold up the remainder of the team. In some circumstances, it may be advantageous to call a temporary halt to the main job to enable others to catch up, so that subsequent jobs which are less weather-dependent can be carried out if weather conditions change. On a small farm, the combine harvester, for example, can be stopped for a short period to enable straw to be baled and carted so that stubble cultivating can take place if and when it rains. Such a hold-up in combining can be built into a cereal cropping system with a proportion of the crop in winter-sown barley. It is possible to take advantage of the break in combining before other varieties are ripe in order to clear straw and begin seed bed preparations for drilling oil seed rape. In large scale organizations, it may be possible to have a number of jobs taking place simultaneously, but on the average-sized holding with a small gang such an opportunity is less likely, so that sequencing of jobs becomes even more important.

Short-term decision-making is a key function in a situation where one operation has to follow another at a very precise time, as with the forage harvester picking up a wilted swath for ensiling into a tower. As the dry matter of the chopped material is so critical, management decisions need to be taken on the spot, involving frequent sampling and subsequent adjustments, particularly to the rate of work of the cutting machinery.

Although many jobs have to be carried out in sequence, each one is a separate operation and the rate of work does not directly affect the others, as, for example, with ploughing, cultivating and drilling. On the other hand, there are many other operations, such as silage-making and most systems of root harvesting, where several jobs link closely together and where overall output is determined by the particular job with the lowest output. Selection of equipment of appropriate size and throughput will minimise such problems, but length of haul or abnormal soil conditions can put a system out of balance and may justify the input of additional, although temporary, resources at any bottle-neck point. This is yet another example of the need for management, perhaps in such a case a foreman, to be out and about adjusting the flow of resources as circumstances change. It is 'management by walking about'. He or she could perhaps drive an additional transport vehicle which still allowed him or her to be regularly in the field and back at the store supervising both ends of the operation. The availability of stand-by equipment and essential items such as spare wheels and replacement hydraulic hose can have a marked effect on throughput, not only in a direct way but also indirectly through the motivation of operators responding to the confidence of having an efficient back-up service.

So much of arable and livestock production involves moving materials from one point to another that transport management is an important component of a manager's job. Managers of large scale industrial operations commonly use the technique of critical path analysis which pinpoints bottle-necks and indicates how best to transform resources and keep vital jobs moving. Few situations in farming necessitate such a formal approach, but the principle of detailed thinking, planning and action is what efficient day-to-day farm management is about.

In farming systems involving a number of enterprises, the problem frequently arises where several jobs must be done at the same time. The making of first-cut silage often clashes with shearing in a dairy and sheep farm, as does spraying with a wide range of jobs on the arable farm. Priorities have therefore to be made and perhaps calculations undertaken to indicate which is the most profitable or critical job. If this becomes a regular problem, then some change to the system may be required such as the use of a different variety or sowing date, or even a change of enterprise.

Many of the examples quoted above refer to field and cropping situations but the operation of livestock enterprises involves similar and often additional considerations. Animals respond well to routine, so that feeding and milking in particular need to be given priority and other tasks fitted into the day as and when convenient. Short diversions from the main task may be sensible in certain circumstances as alternative methods of dealing with the problem would be too expensive. In the small dairy herd, milking will just have to wait if a difficult calving occurs. In the large herd, the early morning milkers can fulfil a valuable role in checking the calving cows before starting to milk. They may even spend a limited time assisting a cow in difficulty but then help must soon be called as considerable milk will be lost by further delay to the main job. Routine tasks, especially in an intensive livestock unit, take up a considerable part of the working day so that it is with some difficulty that other essential, but less routine, jobs have to be carried out. Machinery servicing, building and equipment maintenance are perhaps the best examples of jobs that tend to have a low priority with many stockmen. Naturally and correctly, the animals come first, but constant neglect of other tasks soon leads to inefficiencies. In these circumstances, managers have to effect control, perhaps by providing short-term assistance, to wind up the system and demonstrate how jobs can be carried out more easily if machinery and equipment are well maintained.

None of the issues so far discussed are important in their own right but only in so far as they are subsequently reflected in overall performance. Achieving the objectives of the business involves implementation of the plans which lead to the achievement of previously specified levels of performance. Let us consider, for example, a dairy farmer aiming to calve his replacement heifers at two years of age. In order to achieve the target weight and condition at calving, it is essential to keep the heifers growing well at every stage, as there is just no time for store periods. This involves regular weighing and comparison with targets so that corrective action can be taken in good time. Control of performance is less difficult when the animals are housed, as rapid adjustments can take place to diet or to the environment. It is in the grazing animal that growth rate problems arise, caused by weather conditions, which affect the animals directly and indirectly through forage quality and availability. Standards of husbandry and of grassland management are therefore key factors in sustaining animal performance. Decisions and actions have to be taken on a daily basis in respect of such factors as, nitrogen fertilizer application, movement to alternative grazing or the need to provide supplementary feed. It also involves making judgements as to the expected growth of forage in the weeks ahead.

Plans are made and decisions taken so that satisfactory performance is achieved. Naturally, things often go wrong, and this may be an appropriate point to mention the subject of uncertainty. Uncertainty affects the short-term considerations of operating a farm just as it does the long-term. Yields and prices are subject to uncertainty, but so is the important practical aspect of getting the job done. A wet autumn not only reduces the available days to operate machinery, but it also reduces the rate of work, when machines can get onto the land. In many farms, it may be justifiable to expect that the desired level of performance can be obtained in seven or eight years out of ten. This may be satisfactory, in respect of such considerations as combine harvester capacity in relation to the acreage of cereals to be harvested, as in the difficult years additional capacity can be hired. When rearing dairy heifers to calve at two years of age, however, such uncertainty will be unacceptable. As well-grown animals are such an important input into dairy farming, it may only be acceptable to deal with smaller heifers one year out of ten. In such an occasional circumstances, it may be possible to minimize the number of animals joining the herd by a temporary reduction in the culling rate of older cows. In order to reduce the risk of obtaining low growth rates at pasture, availability of forage should not be a limiting factor, and stocking rates should allow for this with surplus material, in the good growing years, being taken off for conservation. With the continued development of mechanized feeding and manure handling systems, it is expected that there will be a trend away from grazing replacement heifers, as in confinement systems growth rates will be more readily controlled. There are practical and technical ways of contending with uncertainty which supplement the initial choice of enterprises and methods of marketing that managers use to reduce the risks that are an inherent part of the industry.

One remaining point that needs to be considered in respect of operating the farm plan is the question of supervision. We will return to it in our chapter on staff but it cannot be overlooked here. As we have seen, the manager's task is to see that jobs get done on time and to appropriate standards. This is a crucial responsibility of management which we cannot stress too strongly. It involves ensuring that members of staff understand what is expected of them, why the job is necessary and the reasons for doing it in a particular way. Ideally, they will have been involved in setting targets for the particular job, they will have the appropriate tools and other resources and they can be left to get on with the task in hand. That is what good delegation is about, but at the same time managers should be available to assist with the supply of additional resources such as spare parts or extra seed to complete the drilling of a field. Older and more experienced members of staff need less supervision whereas younger trainees require help, advice and encouragement in order to build confidence. Supervision involves knowing when things are in order – but also knowing when they are not – and in knowing what best to do to correct things, whether by careful guidance and watchfulness over staff or by intervening in a way that actually redirects operations and resources.

OUR FINAL THOUGHT

Management is about deciding what you want to do and then doing it. A vital aspect of any production programme lies in determining how much of each enterprise you can actually do. Changes in economic circumstances have always created changes in attitudes about this – and always will.

QUESTIONS AND EXERCISES

- Calculate the gross margins per hectare (or per head for livestock not using land) for every enterprise on your farm.

- Calculate your fixed costs, item by item.

- Using an appropriate combination of the suggested planning procedures (our 'middle' approach) plan your farm.

- Draw up a model of your farm corresponding to that shown in Fig. 7.1.

- Identify, in detail, which of the four kinds of options offer scope for improving profit on your farm.

- Arrange these four options identified in a preferred order and consider how and when each might be pursued.

- Critically review the procedures by which you procure each of the main resources essential to your production system.

- Critically review the supervisory procedures in each of your enterprises.

GUIDE TO FURTHER READING

This is one of the more difficult topics of those featured in this book on which to give references, because of the all-embracing nature of production referred to early in the chapter. Nevertheless, the following reading contains a mixture of a few broadly based texts and some more specifically related to farm production. But the reader will need to keep abreast of contemporary literature on those enterprises/ commodities that concern him.

Barnard, C. S. and Nix, J. S. (1973) *Farm Planning and Control.* Cambridge University Press, Cambridge.
    Chapter 1, pp. 10–13, is a condensed but comprehensive statement about uncertainty.

Drucker, P. F. (1968) *The Practice of Management.* Heinemann, London; Pan Books, London.
Chapter 9 sets the scene on production.

Green, J. R. (1978) How I Manage my Business. *Farm Management* **3** (9) 407–12
This article describes just what the author says it does; an unusually simple and helpful statement about what he is trying to produce and achieve.

Lowe, P. H. (1970) *The Essence of Production.* Pan Books, London.
Unusually, this book really is about production.

Chapter 8

Buying and Selling

An economic view
The farmer's dilemma
A possible answer
Buying
Selling
Market intelligence
Towards a marketing role

AN ECONOMIC VIEW

If production has its complexities, then marketing cannot be far behind. Indeed, there is evidence that many farmers and managers find the whole subject of marketing one of the most perplexing that confronts them. It is not that they do not know how to buy and sell – on the contrary, many of them are very adept at those two things – it is that a clear view of marketing as a discipline, and of their individual role within it, often eludes them. In recent years they have been urged, from professional and political platforms and by the farming press, to 'improve their marketing'. Sometimes this plea has left them even more confused, asking themselves 'just what does that mean; what can I do that I am not already doing?'. We cannot, in one short chapter, answer that question in any detail, even if we had the knowledge applicable to the marketing of all agricultural commodities. Instead, therefore, we have deliberately chosen to offer a fairly general – even philosophical – view of marketing, which may help farmers to understand the subject a little better and to see more clearly where they personally stand in relation to this aspect of their business.

First, we will refer briefly to a simple economic concept: this time it is 'utility'. In economic terms (and we cannot, in any activity which is concerned with resource-use, move very far away from them) utility means the power of a commodity or service to give satisfaction by meeting a need. This means that from the point of view of the consumer, nothing has been finally produced until it has reached the point where it can be purchased and can actually yield satisfaction. Milk, for instance, has not been finally produced until it is on the household table. Potatoes have not been produced until they are in the hands of the consumer, and even then there is some domestic processing to be undertaken before they can literally be consumed. The commercial processes that help to present commodities to the consumer are therefore as much part of the overall production process as the primary production process itself.

All of this means that although, for practical purposes, it is convenient to think of production and marketing as two separate kinds of activity, they are, in fact, all part of the same continuous process of bringing raw materials to the point where they have utility for the consumer. Many writers on the subject take this view quite firmly and it results in marketing being placed alongside production, at the forefront of all industrial activity. Nothing should be produced that is not wanted by somebody else – and so far as food is concerned we exist now in a world in which society is less and less prepared to pay for foods that are surplus to its requirements and more and more inclined to make its demands known. That is why we made specific reference to the requirements of the market in our definition of management in Chapter 2.

Seen in this light, the farmer, while performing a vital early stage in the production–marketing process, is simply one link in a very long chain – albeit one of the earliest links and one without which the others would not exist. Virtually all of a farmer's decisions – especially the major ones relating to the farming programme of the kind that were discussed in the previous chapter – can be seen, ultimately, as marketing decisions as well as production decisions. They help to determine what kind of a link in the chain the farmer forms. To this extent, no matter how perplexing the subject of marketing appears, and no matter how uninvolved or helpless individual farmers feel, they are, in fact, involved. They cannot avoid being so. The fact that they are in business ensures it and they cannot opt out.

THE FARMER'S DILEMMA

Whilst there may be many farmers and farm managers who do not disagree with this economic view of marketing, there are many who, nevertheless, feel in something of a dilemma in this area of their business. The dilemma is this: on the one hand they recognize, increasingly, the inevitability of their involvement; they do, after all, have to buy and sell. They are also aware that, as they seek opportunities to improve or to maintain profit levels, no area of their businesses – and certainly not a major one like marketing – can be ignored. After all, in the systematic approach to reviewing adjustment possibilities, set out in the last chapter, the first kind of possibility concerned increasing gross margins from individual enterprises – and one approach to that could be through seeking better prices for the same commodity or for an improved version of it. No stone should be left unturned and no avenue left unexplored. Farmers with this way of thinking undoubtedly feel the urge to get further involved along the production–marketing chain.

On the other hand, those same farmers often see marketing, with good reason, as a highly professional commercialized activity, conducted – in comparison with the large number of agricultural producers and the even larger number of consumers – by a relatively small number of strong firms that manage the middle ground, the market place. They control the flow of products from the producers to the consumers – depicted in Fig. 8.1 like the pivot of an hourglass.

Faced with this situation, many farmers, with their relatively small businesses, are inclined to the view that it would be difficult – and not even sensible – to try to compete with the commercially strong professionals; so, in the interests of a good division of labour, why try to? Why not concentrate, they say to themselves, on the farmer's real job: that of physical production. That would surely be getting the priorities right – and all managers are urged to do that!

Fig. 8.1. The flow of products from producers to consumers.

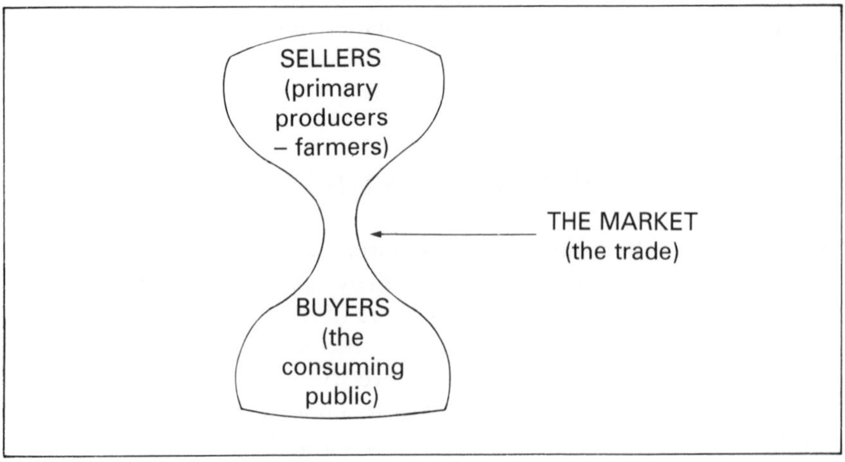

A POSSIBLE ANSWER

This then is the farmer's dilemma; on the one hand a desire on the part of many to get more involved in marketing, but on the other a recognition of strictly limited commercial muscle. Both of these views are understandable, sensible and probably right. We believe that any working answer to the marketing dilemma, as we have described it, will require an acceptance of that view and an acceptance of the compromises that follow from it. The precise answer for any individual will, as we shall see, depend on the nature of his business and his own attitude to it. The main purpose of this chapter is to encourage individuals to develop and recognise what their attitude is.

A major part of the compromise will be to accept that, to a considerable extent, the two apparently conflicting attitudes towards marketing that we have described are both tenable, and that, in a narrowly professional sense, marketing is something best left to the professionals. It involves them in such specialized matters as market research, product identification, the exploration of distribution channels, merchandising, price fixing and adver-tising, a highly technical and commercial set of activities which really are unlikely to concern most farmers or farm managers very much – although we know that there are exceptions. Such activities, however, tend to occur towards the consumer end of our chain of production and the average farmer is unlikely to have the kind of interest, expertise or necessary commercial backing to try to compete in marketing in this sense.

This is not to say, however, that as they diversify – sometimes, for instance, in selling their rural environment and products direct to individual customers, whether tourists or more regular customers – farmers will not be venturing into new areas of marketing where they will not be competing with established trade and industry. In these circumstances, marketing initiatives will need to be taken and an example of what we have in mind will be given later in this chapter.

Diversification or not, however, all farmers are very much involved in the straightforward business of buying and selling – hence the title of this chapter. They owe it to their businesses to try to be as effective in these areas as they try to be in the more practical farming areas. To put it bluntly, when a farmer wants to get hold of some spares for a broken machine, or is trying to decide when to off-load some of the grain harvest, he or she is well and truly involved in the business of marketing. The farmer is operating either as a buyer or a seller. Both activities involve the market – even if the telephone or some other modern means of communication has, for the most part, taken over from the rituals of the traditional market place.

Marketing should be an important part of any farmer's thinking and activity, first in the sense that it is part and parcel of the overall productive process, and secondly because it involves buying as well as selling. It has little to do with those specialized aspects of the marketing profession in which most farmers would be ill-advised to try to compete and probably would not wish to do so. But let us now take a brief look at those two parts of the subject in which they do compete.

BUYING

We have placed buying before selling partly to emphasize that marketing is not confined only to selling and partly because, of the two activities, it is likely to occupy most time. The importance of selling produce on satisfactory terms cannot, of course, be over-emphasized, but for many key farming enterprises and commodities their sale is not a continuous flow, but a series of separate sales, sometimes limited to a small number of transactions a year, following, for example, a harvest. On the other hand the purchase of the many resources that are required in order to farm, will, depending on the system of farming, be incurred much more frequently and much more variously.

The practical aspects of acquiring different kinds of resources have already been discussed in the previous chapter, as part of the production scene. We shall, therefore, satisfy ourselves here with some general comment about the principles involved. There are six requirements that should be met:

---

1. That the commodity or requisite purchased will do the job in question.
2. That the purchase will not only do the job but will meet whatever level of quality is required, either in terms of eventual produce, i.e. crops and livestock, or in terms of a task undertaken, e.g. a repair, or alteration to buildings or machinery.
3. That purchase can be made at a competitive price, given that the first two requirements are met, and that payment can be made by a method and at a time that is mutually acceptable.
4. That, where it is appropriate, some assurance of continued and prompt service can be guaranteed by the supplier.
5. That transactions can be made on a continuing basis, with the maintenance of goodwill on both sides.
6. That satisfaction can be achieved without an undue use of time and effort.

Remembering the simile of the hourglass, farmers will usually be buying in a market – especially at the local level – that has a relatively small number of merchants and suppliers, each probably with more commercial power than any of the individual farmers buying from them. It is in these circumstances that farmers must decide, again, what kind of a link they wish to be in the production–marketing chain. Do they wish to buy as individuals or to become part of a group or co-operative body, accepting the discipline of that body, but also enjoying any of the commercial expertise and power that it will undoubtedly acquire? Bearing in mind that part of his requirements will be to have an assured service with goodwill and without undue effort, it should not be assumed that a small number of suppliers – conjuring up, as it does, the image of the middle man – is necessarily a disadvantage. In many ways, not least in terms of the effort involved in shopping around, it may be a considerable advantage. But it is for each individual purchaser to decide how he deals with those suppliers; and, in particular, whether alone or with others.

SELLING

A word or two now about selling. What we say under this heading follows directly from our contention that the dividing line between production and marketing is a thin one. Basically, we see three different kinds of selling decisions that confront a farmer.

First, at the risk of labouring the point, there are decisions that will more usually be thought of as production decisions, but which have obvious and unavoidable marketing implications. When decisions are made about what commodities to produce, decisions are being made about what will be sold and to whom. When a decision is made about when to produce (e.g. summer or winter milk), a decision is also being made about when to sell, and of course about what costs to incur and what sort of price to accept. When decisions are being made about what quality of goods to produce (e.g. feed or malting barley) then, again, marketing implications ensue relating to different sectors of the market. All of these considerations are directly linked to two of the economic concepts that we have dwelt upon earlier: effective demand in the preceding chapter and utility in this one. No farmer will presumably make decisions to produce anything without good reason to believe that enough individuals will collectively express their effective demand with money, if the commodity in question provides them with utility. Perhaps what is implied, more than anything else, when farmers are urged to improve their marketing is simply that they should be more aware of these consumer considerations. Pressure will increasingly be on them to be so.

Secondly, farmers must decide what kinds of outlets they will use for their produce. Sometimes, in some countries, the commodity itself will determine this for them (e.g. in the UK, milk is sold via the Milk Marketing Board) but frequently a choice will exist: choice in terms of physical outlets and choice in terms of time, i.e. whether to use spot sales or some form of forward contract. Much will still depend on the type of product, and on the attitude of the individual farmer towards considerations of risk.

Finally, we revert to the question 'what kind of link in the chain?'. All farmers will have to decide where to be in the chain and whether to be a link on their own or to act co-operatively with others. Do they wish to limit their involvement in marketing and concentrate their efforts largely on what is conventionally thought of as production? Do they wish to get nearer to the consumer, say, at the farm gate, or in some form of commercially integrated activity? Do they wish to go it alone or accept the advantages and disadvantages of combined effort? How many eggs do they want, in how many baskets? What are the possibilities? These are the questions farmers should ask themselves.

An example of buying

The procurement of straw for an all-grass dairy farm will be taken as an example of the need for a management input to ensure the efficient buying of a required commodity.

The introduction of cubicle housing to many such farms has reduced the quantity of material required for bedding purposes but developments in machinery and ration formulation have increased the popularity of straw for feeding to cows and youngstock. Numerous factors need to be taken into account to obtain the appropriate quantity, type and quality of material, delivery time and cost. These include:

1. Usage   – Direct feeding; long or for chopping
                  – Feeding after chemical treatment
                  – Bedding; direct from bale or for shredding
                  – Temporary walling, e.g. for sugar beet clamps.
2. Type   – Wheat, barley, oat or thrashed herbage seed variety may be significant if for feed usage.
3. Bale Shape – Increasing in range following baler developments
    (**a**) Traditional small – Preferable for use in cubicles, calf houses and feeding racks; more effort required in stacking.
    (**b**) Round   – Suitable for bedding, covered yards or feeding from ring-mangers; possible to store in the open, difficult to transport.
    (**c**) Large high   – Much cheaper to transport; heavy duty loader
         density   essential for handling; preferable for use in large yards and as temporary walls.
    (**d**) Medium sized – More flexible but also convenient to transport,
         high density   well suited to enable high throughput from

treatment machines, important if contractors charge on an hourly basis.
4. Delivery time – In most years, material available throughout the year but alternatives.
   (a) Ex-field at harvest – Usually lowest cost, especially for ready payment, therefore cash needed; quality may be suspect if baled damp; storage ideally undercover; less flexibility in specifying actual time of delivery, so possible clash with other tasks.
   (b) As required – Preferable if storage facilities are limited; quality more dependable but price usually higher.
   (c) Flexible – Especially to suit the vendor; contractor may value the order and deliver when spare vehicles available; quality should be ensured if delivered from barn storage. Price will be influenced by payment terms.

It can be seen that considerable information will be required to plan and make decisions as to the optimum straw requirements. Having adequate stocks in store at all times, but especially during periods of high usage, should avoid any concern about being without supplies. Such a situation, if only for a short period, could lead to numerous problems, e.g. dirty cows, increased mastitis, feeding more expensive commodities. Control of supply, quality and price are therefore essential aspects of the management of the buying process.

An example of selling

The sale of cull cows from a dairy herd will be used as an example of the benefits to be obtained from a management input into this activity.

Cows are culled from dairy herds for numerous reasons. Surveys of producers indicate that only one in three cases results from a decision to cull due to low yield, low milk compositional quality, old age, behavioural problems or poor confirmation. Two out of three cases therefore, are unplanned, i.e. the cow is affected by disease such as infertility, mastitis or lameness and so retention in the herd is not feasible. The majority of milk producers treat their culls very much as a byproduct, selling them immediately a problem arises and making no effort to add value to the product. An increasing number, however, are putting more effort into increasing the sale price of their culls and so adding to the profitability of the herd. When cull cows make a higher price, there is more justification for increasing the culling rate within the herd, so allowing it to benefit from such factors as improved genetic potential of the incoming heifers (assuming the best available bulls are being used), reduced mastitis (removing chronic cases) or improved staff morale (removing problem cows).

The price received for a cull cow depends upon three main factors:

1. Time of sale – seasonal price changes show a well established pattern in the UK, with highest prices being in the spring when supplies on the market are at the lowest level. As the most popular months for calving are in autumn and early winter, the peak of cull sales take place in the autumn at the end of lactation and before the need for winter housing.

2. Weight of animal – although dependent upon breed, type and age, the highest prices are obtained for heavier animals which produce a higher yield of saleable meat from the carcass. There are three recognized grades of cull cow:

Grade 1 – good quality, killing-out percentage over 50 (i.e. % of live weight as carcass). These are often suitable for the export trade.

Grade 2 – fair quality, less than 50% killing-out, well suited to manufactured products, e.g. meat pies.

Grade 3 – poor quality, only suitable for boning-out for low value products.

It can be seen that as the heavier cows are also worth more per kilogramme, the returns from such animals shows a considerable premium:

Grade	Average weight (kg)	Average price (p/kg)	Cow value (£)
1	600	100	600
2	500	85	425
3	400	75	310

3. Marketing method – a high proportion of culls are sold for traditional reasons at auction markets. Prices tend to be marginally improved at those markets where weighing takes place prior to sale. Direct sale to the abattoir is preferred by those producers who, for humane reasons, wish to avoid their cattle having the unnecessary stress of an additional journey to one or more markets. An increasing number of producer groups are being formed with the aim of better matching of supply to demand. Loads of similar type animals are directed to the most appropriate outlet, following skilled selection by a fieldsman from the group.

There are therefore numerous ways in which the milk producer can add value to his cull cows.

1. Identifying potential culls at an early date so as to plan feeding, grazing or housing and sale date in order to optimize returns. An autumn calver with, for example, low butterfat production, can be left unserved, the level of nutrition towards the end of the winter increased with sale taking place in the spring to coincide with the seasonable peak of prices.

2. Communicating regularly with potential buyers, e.g. abattoirs or a co-operative, indicating that a number of animals of a specified type are in the pipeline. These can then be transferred to slaughter at a mutually satisfactory time, e.g. to make up an export order.

3. If feed stocks and accommodation are available, it usually pays to retain animals which would normally go to slaughter at the end of the grazing season until prices increase. Capital is obviously tied up in this activity and if the cow is not milking, feed for maintenance as well as fattening will be required. The major benefit comes if the grade of animal can be increased, e.g. Grade 2 to 1.

Table 8.1 indicates the likely effect of retaining a potential cull in the herd for 3 months and increasing the diet by 1.5 kg concentrates per day. It indicates the importance of the date of sale.

4. Cash flow considerations may override many of the above factors. If credit limits are a concern, income from culls, even at less than optimal values, could well be an essential input to the business, it is interesting to note that the most profitable dairy farms not only produce milk most efficiently, but also obtain the best prices for calves and cull cows. Managers of

Table 8.1. The effect of retaining a potential cull in the herd for 3 months.

Finishing period	Nov–Feb	Feb–May	Aug–Nov
Initial liveweight (kg)	500	500	500
price (p/kg)	70	80	82
value (£)	350	400	410
Final liveweight (kg)	550	550	550
price (p/kg)	85	90	75
value (£)	467	495	412
Increase in value (£)	117	95	2
Extra feed cost (£)	20	20	20
Margin (£)	97	75	−18
Plus increase if grade increases 10p/kg	55	55	55
Margin (£)	152	130	37
Less interest 16% for 3 months	14	16	17
Net margin	138	114	20

such enterprises must identify the needs of the particular market outlet and take effective action to their production to best meet the needs of that market – that is good selling.

MARKET INTELLIGENCE

This chapter would not be complete without specific reference to the important question of market intelligence data and the part that they play in marketing decisions.

The major difficulty about all such decisions is that they have to be made at a given point of time in respect to circumstances that will exist at some future point in time. This can be a particular problem in farming, especially where the length of the production cycle is long, but also because of the generally long term nature of any commitment to specialize in the production of one or another agricultural enterprise. Capital and expertise quickly become relatively fixed – a problem which is at the root of all investment decisions, as we shall see in the next chapter.

It has often been said that successful marketing means having the right commodity, at the right place, at the right price and at the right time. But decisions do have to be made now in order that this can be done later on – and, as we saw in the chapter on decision making, having information is an important part of that process. Some of the information that is necessary will relate to circumstances that already exist on the farm in question, for example records of past (and therefore expected) physical performance levels. To this kind of information, however, will have to be added the best possible estimates that can be made of future prices and costs, both in the short and the long term.

So important is this subject, that a whole chapter has been devoted, towards the end of the book, to the matter of acquiring information. In the meantime, however, we see two fundamentally different kinds of decisions which have to be made, for which some indication of market circumstances may be helpful.

First, there are decisions about what enterprises to be in; whether to expand, or contract, whether to get in or to get out. Such decisions are strategic in nature and tend not to be made too often – indeed, it may be dangerous if they are. Sometimes they are made for non-economic reasons, as, for instance, when an ageing farmer decides to quit a physically demanding enterprise like milk production. To the extent, however, that an eye must be kept on likely changes in effective demand, it is wise for farmers and farm managers, wherever they are, to keep abreast of any available 'situation' and 'outlook' material as well as responsible comment on such matters as national and international production trends and economic forecasts, not to mention political events, and relevant scientific and technical developments. We appreciate that this is a tall order. Much of this kind of information may not be readily available or readily quantifiable and, because of the inherent uncertainty and interactions of world affairs, may be overtaken by subsequent events. It would be unwise for a farmer to use this kind of material to make hasty or constant changes to his or her farming systems and methods. We do, however, believe that farmers are likely to make better long term strategic decisions if they are informed about these matters than if they are not. If it only serves to convince them that they are doing the right things, and to encourage them to go on doing them as well as they can, it will have been an invaluable exercise. But occasionally the situation will be otherwise and, looking ahead to the single market in Europe as the 1990s unfold and both new opportunities and fresh competition appears, the need to be alert and responsive to need for strategic change will become more important.

The second kind of decision for which commercial information can be helpful is much more short term. The farming press, local radio, producer organizations, personal observation and information obtained directly on request to the trade, may all be of help. The question here will not be related to the adjustment of enterprises or farm systems, but to the disposal of produce from existing enterprises. The fact that there is a choice – to dispose now or later – implies, of course, that we are concerned here either with non-perishable supplies or with livestock that may be taken on. In a nutshell, the question to be answered is 'does one sell (or buy) now or later?'. So far as selling is concerned there will usually be some cost of waiting: feeding stuffs, storage, interest charges, and, of course, any lost opportunities (economists talk literally about 'opportunity cost') from locked-up capital. But there may also be gain from waiting, in the form of higher prices. This is a situation for the use of a partial budget in which potential gains and potential losses can be weighed against each other. The word 'potential' has deliberately been used here because neither set of information – especially the returns – can be guaranteed. Nevertheless, decisions have to be made. It is impossible to defer indefinitely; remember, to do nothing is to do something. Sooner or later the best possible estimate must be made, and, as with more long-term decisions, it is surely better to have some information, especially from the more reputable sources, than to have none. In the last resort, however, these are the questions on which farmers have to make their own judgements and they may rely as much on their intuitive 'feel' for situations as on any formal analysis of trends, however sophisticated or crude that may be. This may be increasingly the case as farmers venture into new 'minority' enterprises and activities of a non-farming nature when the availability of the kind of traditional market information that we have talked about above may simply not be available. More and more we envisage the farmer having to go out and look for new market opportunities, not relying on being told about them. He or she will need to spend time – a necessary prerequisite for success in any aspect of management – to cultivate ideas and contacts in order to exploit his or her own set of comparative advantages. At the same time realistic farmers and farm managers know that they cannot win all the time and that they need to have a proper regard for goodwill and mutual trust in their dealings with others.

Finally, we should say that in discussing both the outlook data relevant to long-term situations and short-term market intelligence data we have carefully expressed the view that such information may help in the appropriate decision situations. We do not know that it will, and there is always the possibility that if too many make the right decision, their combined effect on supply and demand will make it the wrong one. We cannot allow ourselves, however, to believe that worse decisions are likely to be made when there is access to such information, compared with when there is not. What we do believe, is that good decisions do not automatically follow from having market information available, however good it may be. Good decisions embrace so much more.

TOWARDS A MARKETING ROLE

At the outset of this chapter we made it clear that we did not intend to try to provide answers to individual marketing problems. We believe, however, that farmers and farm managers find the subject of marketing a perplexing one and that their own attitude is often unclear, if not inconsistent. We have therefore offered a series of thoughts intended to help individuals, first, to get the subject into perspective, and secondly, to see more clearly their own role within it.

---

1. That farmers may not always be 'in' marketing in an aggressive, professional sense – although increasingly, especially as they diversify, they will need to take initiatives that previously they have not.
2. They are nevertheless always in marketing whether they know it or not, and whether they like it or not.
3. All business decisions which relate to production (and sooner or later most of them do) are also marketing decisions.
4. Room for manoeuvre in marketing is largely dictated by farming enterprises and by personal attitudes to independence and risk; but even to recognize that there may not be much room for manoeuvre is to recognize a marketing reality.
5. Buying goods and services is as much part of marketing as selling them, and timely delivery can be vital.
6. A serious effort should be made by farmers to understand the structure,

functions and services of those marketing institutions – government and commercial – with which they are concerned, whether in a commercial, regulatory or a developmental way.

7. All areas of a business should be explored in any endeavour to increase or improve profits and, depending on personal objectives and business circumstances, this may or may not include marketing. As a rule, it should; and as a rule it will be more helpful to have some information with which to help make decisions rather than not to have any.

Taking a long-term view of this whole subject, we see that the service element in the economy has been increasing over a good many years, while, with a growing division of labour, primary producers have become more and more removed from the final consumer. But we see also a growing desire (in the UK at least) on the part of farmers to become re-involved nearer to the point of the consumer, both in conventional farming and less conventional activities. Farm shops are but one example of this. It has always been true, however, that distant fields can look greener, and as marketing in the professional sense becomes increasingly sophisticated and concentrated in large concerns, we wonder how much scope really exists for farmers to accept the opportunities and risks associated with this sector. Apart from 'marketing' the environment, which farmers are uniquely placed to do, scope may well be limited to those who have the appropriate personal and commercial aptitudes and flair. This does not mean, however, that farmers are not and cannot be involved in marketing. The whole of this chapter, indeed, has been to suggest the contrary. Some, however, will clearly be more involved than others. What is important is that all farmers should understand clearly what marketing role they play.

OUR FINAL THOUGHT

If nobody sells, nothing happens!

QUESTIONS AND EXERCISES

- Read through the final section of this chapter again and then decide what your own marketing role should be.

- Make some spot checks (e.g. for a week at a time) on how you use your time. Identify what proportion of it is spent in marketing. Then ask yourself if this is enough, and, if not, decide what you can or should do about it.

- Taking each of your existing enterprises in turn, and with appropriate help from others, carry out a thorough review of your marketing methods and then take whatever action seems necessary.

- Periodically carry out a feasibility study for *one* new enterprise or activity that you might add to your business – taking full regard of its market potential.

- Make the effort to read any one of the references on marketing which follows: the CCAHC booklet would be a good one to start with.

GUIDE TO FURTHER READING

A Director's Guide to Practical Marketing (1982) Central Council for Agricultural and Horticultural Co-operation.
  A valuable and entertaining first read for anyone wanting to get more involved in this subject.

Barker, J. W. (1981) *Agricultural Marketing.* Oxford University Press, Oxford.
  A readable and helpful introduction to the marketing framework.

Bateman, D. I. (ed.) (1972) *Marketing Management in Agriculture.* Dept. of Agricultural Economics, University College of Aberystwyth.
  A valuable survey of the subject.

Farm Management (1972) **2**, No. 3; (1974) **2**, No. 8; and (1975–76) **3**, No. 1.
  Three issues of the CMA journal, each of which contains a number of helpful articles on marketing.

Kiam, V. (1986) *Going For It.* Collins, London.
  Sub-titled 'how to succeed as an entrepreneur' and therefore strongly market-oriented.

O'Connell, D. and Purser, K. (1988) *A Farm For All Seasons*, 2nd edn. Rural Investigations, Highworth, Wilts.
  Valuable information on a wide range of 'new' farm-based enterprises and activities.

Slee, B. (1987) *Alternative Farm Enterprises.* Farming Press Ltd, Ipswich.
  A good, methodical review, with strong marketing emphasis and one chapter directly on the subject.

Turner, J. and Taylor, M. (1989) *Applied Farm Management.* BSP Professional Books, Oxford.
  Much stronger on marketing than most comparable books.

Chapter 9

Finance

Capital and farming
A way of looking at financial management
Some important omissions
Accounts – The profit and loss account
– Inputs and outputs
– Comparative analysis
– Enterprise accounts: gross and net margins
Budgets – Complete budgets
– Partial budgets
– Break even budgets
– Cash flows
Balance sheets – Structure and meaning of a balance sheet
– Balance sheet ratios
– Return on existing capital
Investment appraisal – The importance of fresh investment
– Appraisal methods
– Investment checklist

CAPITAL AND FARMING

In keeping with the central theme of this book, the purpose of this chapter is not to spell out in detail the mechanics of all known financial management techniques, but to comment on their meaning and use in the context of farming.

There is quite definitely something frightening about this subject. No farmer or manager needs to be told of its importance, but it is an aspect of farm management from which many shy away. Farmers are not unique in this respect. One farmer said to us, when asked why he co-operated in an annual farm accounts scheme, 'Because, whether I like it or not, once a year I have to sit down and discuss things that I might otherwise avoid'.

There are various understandable reasons for this kind of attitude. Financial matters can be complicated; they involve mathematics, and even at an elementary level that can produce mental blockages for many of us. Terminology is not always clearly defined, especially in the hands of amateurs; it can be a barrier to communication rather than an aid. And, of course, figures, when they are accurate, sometimes present a cold and unpalatable truth, and who wants to come face to face with that too often?

The situation as we have described it above may be changing, but in our view only gradually, and we are anxious to stick to basics and avoid over-complication. We would like to encourage confidence in an area of management where it is often lacking, and as a first step it will perhaps help to recognize an essential difference between the way an economist regards capital and the way most people in business do. To the economist, capital is one of three separate factors of production, together with land and labour. Each has its own characteristics and its reward. Capital, in this context, represents deferred consumption; a stock of resources produced in some previous time period, to be used to satisfy future wants, e.g. machinery, buildings, livestock, seeds and fertilizers. To the average person in business, however, capital is something less precisely defined. It simply means the monetary value of his or her productive resources – whether he owns them or acquired them with borrowed money, and whether he uses them up on the spot or retains them. This is an absolutely reasonable view to take. We should keep it in mind, and it will help to eliminate some of the mystique that can otherwise surround the notion of capital. This simplified view of capital should also help to bring the subject right into the heart of practical farming itself, rather than to leave it as some sort of appendage to be nervous of. Using resources is, after all, what farm management is about. By definition, therefore – the businessman's definition, not the economist's – using capital equates with farming, and financial management is concerned with acquiring that capital, with using it and with maintaining it.

A WAY OF LOOKING AT FINANCIAL MANAGEMENT

We can now move on to look at the nuts and bolts of financial management. This could be approached in many different ways and there is nothing sacrosanct about the approach that we propose to adopt, except that it is simple. It is depicted in the two-way diagram shown in Fig. 9.1. This diagram is based on the simple assumption that the subject can be subdivided both in content and in time into two parts. So far as content is concerned there are: (a) those aspects of financial management that are to do with day-to-day trading activities, and (b) those that are more to do

Fig. 9.1. The structure of financial management.

	Past and the present	Future
Trading	RECORDS AND ACCOUNTS	BUDGETS
Capital	BALANCE SHEETS	INVESTMENT APPRAISAL

with the state of play in the business at particular points of time, i.e. with its capital status. So far as time is concerned, there are: (a) considerations which relate to the present and the recent past (we find it difficult to differentiate between the two because the moment something happens it becomes part of the recent past), and (b) considerations which concern the future.

This view of things results in the four segments in Fig. 9.1. The top left-hand segment (recent and past trading) is primarily concerned with accounts and with the records that make them possible. The top right-hand segment (future trading) is concerned with various forms of budgets. Then turning to the capital side of things, the bottom left-hand segment (past capital) relates to balance sheets, while the bottom right-hand one concerns investment appraisal. Under each of these four headings (accounts, budgets, balance sheets and investment appraisal) there are numerous techniques and topics that make up the whole. Some of these issues have already been mentioned in other chapters. At the risk of some duplication, however, it seems necessary to briefly comment here on those aspects of the subject with which every farmer and farm manager should be reasonably conversant. This does not mean that they need to be a financial wizard. But it does mean that they should have a clear view of what the relevant concepts and procedures mean, to the extent that in several of the more straightforward areas of the subject they are capable of manipulating the relevant figures on their own. The itemized version of our diagram indicates the topics that will be discussed.

Fig. 9.2. Detailed structure of financial management.

	Past and present	Future
Trading	ACCOUNTS whole farm accounts (and records) inputs and outputs comparative analysis gross margins net margins	BUDGETS complete partial breakeven and sensitivity cash flows
Capital	BALANCE SHEETS structure and meaning ratios return on 'existing' capital	INVESTMENT APPRAISAL incremental capital rate of return pay back discounting investment checklist

SOME IMPORTANT OMISSIONS

Before proceeding, it should be said that there are certain important topics which, for reasons given in Chapter 1, have not been commented on. In particular these include questions of company law and structure, inheritance and taxation. These topics require legal expertise which we do not have; they are shaped and influenced by particular national legislation and are subject, also, to constant change. In choosing to omit them we are not unmindful of their supreme importance, especially in the matter of main-taining business capital intact. We strongly advise all farmers and managers to employ, and cultivate, the appropriate professionals to advise them in these specialized matters. Such people are not commonly to be found amongst the general run of agricultural advisers and consultants. Very often, we fear, they are not easy to find amongst the more professional ranks either. There are many accountants, even in rural areas, for whom farmers constitute a relatively small share of their total custom and who lack any deep expertise in farming finance. Too often, for instance. it seems to us that 'tax planning' boils down to the statement 'you look like making a good profit this year, what about replacing a tractor?' And too often farmers seem to be at the end of the queue for the speedy completion of accounts. The remedy, of course, is in their own hands, but that is another story.

ACCOUNTS

The profit and loss account

Interpreting a profit and loss account is not as straightforward as it might appear. It is perhaps not too surprising, therefore, that we have met a number of farmers who are inclined to shy away from it. In fact, it does what its name implies: it gives an account of a year's trading and shows the profit or loss. Strictly speaking a trading account and a profit and loss account are two different things, the former relating only to trading items directly associated with the main activity of the business in question, and the latter indicating final profit (or loss) after certain 'below the line' items of an overhead nature (e.g. finance charges, grants etc.) have been taken into consideration. Very often, however, especially in small businesses, the terms are interchangeable, and the niceties of terminology should not worry us here. What is important is what the account tells us, i.e. what profit or loss has been incurred and how it came about.

Profit, for any particular time period, is a measurement of the difference between the value of all the resources used in that time period, and the value of everything that was or could have been sold. To the extent that a business is a continuing operation, a trading account is rather like a slice of a cake. Sturrock (see Further Reading), in what is still one of the best and most under-praised of the books on farm accounting, suggests that the notion is best understood by imagining that a farmer 'buys in' his valuation (from himself) on the opening day of the financial year and then continues to buy in resources during the year. He also sells produce during the year and 'sells out' the valuation (again to himself) on the last day. Opening and closing creditors and debtors must be taken into account, and profit, in this sense, is then the difference between all selling and all buying, the 'value added' to the resources that were there at the beginning of the year or bought in during it. In those countries where tax is based on profits, it will be based on this figure, even though a large part of it may be locked up in valuations; one day they will be released. The normal layout of a trading or profit and loss account will, therefore, look like this:-

Opening valuation	Receipts
Expenses	Closing Valuation

Profit	Loss

It is this basic understanding of what profit means that we emphasize here. There are however two other important, and at first sight rather confusing, points to be added. First, it is in the nature of accountancy that, surprising as it may seem, no trading account can be guaranteed to be exactly accurate. In the preparation of accounts, conventions have to be employed to allow, for instance, for non-cash items like machinery depreciation, and for the valuation of produce and resources on hand. There is a tendency to be conservative in these matters so as not to anticipate profit that in the event may not accrue and, from time to time, conventions get changed. No farmer, for instance, who has replaced machinery and equipment in recent years will be in any doubt about the realities of replacement cost as opposed to historic cost, but accountants still have no uniform approach to 'inflation accounting' methods. We would recommend the reader who wishes to become conversant with the details of inflation accounting to read the chapter on 'accounting for inflation', in Warren's book referred to at the end of Chapter 2.

There is, then, no such thing as an exactly true statement of profit; there is only a 'true and fair view' depending upon the conventions and method used, and our second point of difficulty concerns the unravelling of that true and fair view of things in order to make judgements about the efficiency – or lack of it – within the different sectors of a farm business. A trading account in its raw state is less help in this than might be imagined. There are two main reasons for this. First, the amount of detail shown in trading accounts is invariably inadequate; perhaps because inadequate records have been kept in the first place, perhaps because important items of cost of revenue, or of valuation, have been lumped together by the accountant simply because there is no statutory need to give them in anything like full detail. Some of the calculations that one would like to make are not possible without additional detail – and it may not be there unless asked for.

The second main difficulty in using a trading account for management purposes – i.e. for 'management accounting', as opposed to straightforward 'financial accounting' (i.e. the *reporting* of results) – is that in its normal format, information relating to particular enterprises or particular inputs is scattered throughout the document some perhaps in the receipts, some in the expenditure and some in either of the valuations.

Returning to the layout of a trading account shown above, a statement which gave us the information in the example below would tell us only that the annual profit was £10,000, on an average capital value of £52,500 with sales of £105,000. It is a statement of result. We may, by making appropriate comparisons, begin to make some judgements about that result but we are in no position (even if substantially more detail were provided) to begin to make serious judgements about efficiency.

	£		£
Opening valuation	50,000	Receipts	105,000
Expenses	100,000	Closing valuation	55,000
Profit	10,000		
	160,000		160,000

It is, in fact, virtually impossible to look at a trading account in this form and state – especially where livestock are involved – and to deduce with any accuracy what is happening. Some unravelling is required, some adjustments need to be made and some extra (physical) information introduced before we can talk about inputs and outputs and the efficiency with which the one is converted into the other. It is to this that we now turn.

Inputs and outputs

In order to fully understand the terms input and output we need to get away from the ideas of expenditure and sales. An input is the measure of how much of a resource is actually *used* in a given time period, whether or not it was paid for in that time period or indeed, as in the case of family labour, whether it has an actual charge to it at all. Similarly, output is a measure of production in a given time period whether or not what was produced was actually sold. Valuations at the beginning and the end therefore form an important part of both concepts.

The conventional headings under which farm trading accounts are converted into statements of input and output, and the calculations involved, are as follows:

Inputs	**Outputs**
(opening valuation +	(closing valuation +
expenditure) −	sales) − (opening
(closing valuation)	valuation + purchases)

These simple formulae can be applied to each principal item (or groups of items) of input and output. The normal conventions are as follows, with seven headings on each side of the account:

Inputs	Outputs
Bought feed	Crops
Bought seed	Milk
Fertilizer	Cattle
Rent and rates	Sheep
Power and machinery	Pigs
Wages	Poultry
Sundries	Sundries

It is not our intention to discuss in detail either the arithmetic that is involved in this process or the kinds of recording and book keeping systems that are required in order to make this kind of analysis possible. Suffice to say that when manually operated it all begins with the making of careful notes on the stubs of cheque books and bank paying-in books of the type shown below:

On cheque stubs

Date	Purchased from	Product	Quantity	Price paid

On paying-in stubs

Date	Received from	Produce	Quantity	Price received

These should then be transferred into an appropriately headed cash analysis book. When computerized, the same basic process of recording and allocating is involved, simply using a different system of book-keeping. Armed then with the summaries for the year and the necessary valuations it is a simple matter to calculate, for example, that the output from livestock enterprise 'A' in the year in question amounted to £100,000:

	£
Closing valuation	30,000
Sales	100,000
Subtotal	130,000
Less:	
Opening valuation	20,000
Purchases	10,000
Subtotal	30,000
Output	100,000

Similarly, use of input X (perhaps bought food consumed by enterprise A) might have amounted to £60,000:

	£
Opening Valuation	5,000
Expenditure	65,000
Subtotal	70,000
Less:	
Closing Valuation	10,000
Input	60,000

We have now moved some way towards being able to say something about an important element of this enterprise, i.e. the conversion of food into livestock output – although we do not yet know the size of the enterprise in terms of number of animals nor do we know at this stage whether home-grown as well as purchased food had been consumed.

In order, therefore, to arrive at the true measure of the total levels of output from each enterprise and the total quantity of inputs that have been absorbed by them, it must be remembered that the trading account does not necessarily tell the whole story. Quite apart from the falsifying effect of contra accounts i.e. one item being traded against another – which must be carefully watched and allowed for – allowances may be needed for the transference of items between enterprises (for example, the transfer of young stock from a breeding to a livestock rearing unit) which, so far as the trading account is concerned, simply do not appear. The extent to which such transfers need to be allowed for will depend on how fine a breakdown of enterprise output is required. There can, however, be no ignoring the fact that if cereals are grown and consumed by livestock on the farm, the cereals need to be credited and the food bill debited with the amount involved. If, for example, in the livestock valuation shown above £10,000 worth of homegrown grains had been fed to the enterprise, the food conversion ratio (i.e. food costs per £100 of output) would have been 70 not 60, as the first figures suggested.

Coupled, therefore, with a limited amount of basic physical information about the farm in question – its cropping and stocking and, most important, an allocation of concentrated feed between livestock enterprises – these measurements of inputs and outputs can then be used in a variety of ways to test past performance and possible future decisions. Typical of such measurements would be outputs per productive unit (e.g. crop output per hectare, and livestock output per animal) and inputs per productive unit (e.g. food costs per £100 of output). In this way, raw financial data from the trading account – by itself and in its original form not very helpful – can be transformed into useable management accounting data for use in 'account' and 'comparative' analysis which we now go on to discuss. We encourage anyone who is managing a farm to become adept – if they are not already – in the manipulation and interpretation of accounting data in this way.

Comparative analysis

Comparative analysis is the name generally given to the technique of comparing the financial results from one farm with the average results from a group of similar farms.

The main criticisms of comparative analysis in the past have been that no two farms are alike, that averaged results on a sample of farms (however similar) do not represent any real situation at all, and that management decisions are concerned with the effect of marginal adjustments within individual enterprises rather than with averaged results over the whole farm.

We accept these criticisms in strict academic terms. But if agriculture is guilty of using this technique it is in good company: it is much used in various forms throughout the business world. In that real world, crude tools are often necessary. We defend a limited use of the technique on the grounds that averages do provide an indication of the level towards which results in any given population tend, that it is natural for individuals to wonder where they stand in relation to that average, and that, unless in totally untutored hands, the general questioning of performances prompted by this exercise is unlikely to be other than beneficial. It is also true that if judgements about performance are to be made at all – and how can that be avoided? – some form of comparison must inevitably be made against a yardstick. Where that yardstick can be derived from established knowledge of technical performance levels within individual enterprises, all well and good. Where, however, whole-farm judgements are required, yardsticks or 'standards' are likely to be available only from whole-farm financial surveys of the kind used in comparative analysis.

It is of course important that when such comparisons are made, like is compared with like and that the calculations have conceptual meaning. Certain adjustments usually have to be made to trading account data before inter-farm comparisons can be made. In particular, allowances need to be made for the value of any unpaid labour that is being employed, and distortions resulting from ownership and management charges (rents, mortgages, interest, management salaries etc.) must be avoided. We would simply say here that it is important if individual figures are being compared with published data that the basis for those data is clearly understood and the necessary allowances made. It is largely for this reason that the agricultural economists' measure of Management and Investment Income (i.e. the return to management and investment before any charges are made against profit for those two items) retains its value and popularity. It is not (as is sometimes thought) that agricultural economists fail to recognize the importance of interest and management charges where they exist before final profit is arrived at in any particular case, but for the reasons indicated, valid comparisons may have to be made before that stage in the calculations is reached.

Calculations must also be conceptually meaningful, which means that they must involve inputs and outputs that are logically related to each other. For example, milk output per cow has meaning; so do milk output per hectare devoted to dairying, sheep output per ewe, pig output per sow, wheat output per hectare of wheat, fertilizer use per hectare, and labour and machinery costs per hectare. All of these figures have been related to the units (either livestock or land) from which they have been derived, and the input figures have been related to the units which absorb them. By contrast, input: output ratios make no sense when the dividend and the divisor have no logical relationship: when, for example, the output from one enterprise, occupying *part* of a farm, is expressed per hectare of the *whole* farm (e.g. sheep output per hectare of the whole farm, when they occupy only part of it) or when an input is not properly related to the production unit that absorbs it (e.g. concentrated feed per hectare, instead of per consuming livestock unit). If these kinds of calculations are used in comparative analysis the technique, not unnaturally, falls into disrepute.

There are obvious dangers that can arise on any particular farm from examining individual efficiency measures of this type in isolation, and from drawing too many conclusions without reference to the rest of the farm's economy. Ideally one would wish to examine all inter-related measures simultaneously, but in practice this is clearly not possible. One has to start somewhere. We suggest that a logical starting point is to begin with the profit: that, after all, is the main purpose of the exercise.

It is helpful to begin this kind of exercise with a few simple all-embracing calculations and then to home-in in more detail on where the problems seem to be. The following very simplified example might, for instance, be a good starting point.

	Your Farm	Local Average (£ per hectare)	Difference
Total enterprise output	1,000	1,050	−50
Less variable costs	400	380	+20
Total gross margin	600	670	−70
Less fixed costs	570	470	+100
Management, Investment Income	30	200	−170

In this situation, with profits well below average, attention is immediately drawn to the existence of above-average fixed costs, and the reasons for these would need to be explored at an early stage. There may be (probably are) other matters to be examined, however, and a systematic approach is advised. We suggest the kind of sequence illustrated in Fig. 9.2

– starting with profit and the overall difference between output and costs – before moving on to consider those aspects of the farm where adjustment may be most possible, looking first at those factors which affect overall production levels (yields, prices and system intensity) and then at the more adjustable items of cost (feedingstuffs, labour and machinery). If the data being examined are cast in terms of gross margins and fixed costs the procedure need not differ in essence from this one.

Fig. 9.3. Comparative analysis of efficiency.

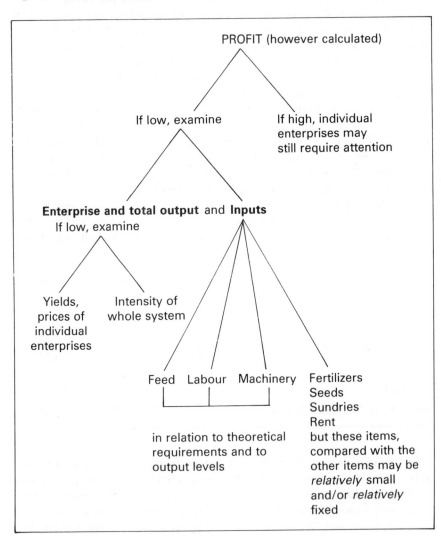

Before moving on from this topic we must say that too often, in our view, this type of systematic analysis is reserved for situations in which profits have disappointed, when it could usefully be applied as a routine tool of financial management. No one would claim that comparative analysis is a sophisticated tool, without limitations, but we believe that it is a worthwhile annual habit to adopt.

Enterprise accounts: gross and net margins

Before moving on to consider the budgeting section of this whole subject it is appropriate to offer comment on the subject of enterprise accounts. We deliberately use the word 'accounts' here, rather than 'costs', so as not to confuse what we have in mind with full enterprise costings traditionally undertaken in many countries by agricultural economists, principally to provide evidence for price-fixing discussions. So far as the farm manager is concerned we believe that the approach is likely to be more detailed than is usually necessary (although there may be exceptions) and because of the arbitrariness with which shared costs are sometimes allocated between enterprises, it may even lead to positively misleading conclusions.

Gross margins have gone a long way towards meeting farm management needs in this respect, but perhaps not all the way. Certainly the use of profit and loss accounts becomes more pertinent to the kind of judgements and decisions that managers have to make, the more they reveal information about individual enterprises. If they contain sufficient detail, profit and loss accounts can be manipulated so that something close to the true gross margins for each enterprise can be calculated. This requires, however, that the full output from each separate enterprise can be identified – including the transfer of items between enterprises such as grain grown to feed on the farm – and also that sufficiently detailed records are separately kept to enable the variable costs of each enterprise to be identified. The main requirement here is that good records exist of the use of concentrated feed. More often than not reasonable estimates, or even a resort to the use of standard data, might be sufficient for the other items.

It is a fact, however, that gross margins only tell part of the story. Although they provide a measure of enterprise efficiency, they are by definition only partial enterprise accounts. They exclude any consideration of the fixed costs that are absorbed by the enterprises in question, and furthermore they cannot take into account any complementarity that may exist between enterprises; the contribution, for instance, that a livestock grazing enterprise may make to subsequent arable crops occupying the same land. All of this means that gross margins must be interpreted with care. They have their definite uses; they also have their limitations. In particular it should be remembered that, on a mixed farm, different enterprises make different calls on the fixed costs. Any notion that fixed costs can be equally and meaningfully spread over the whole land area of a farm, and that the gross margin from each enterprise should then be expected to cover that cost, is both false and misleading. There are obvious examples amongst the less intensive grassland enterprises, where a low gross margin per hectare is entirely acceptable on the grounds that it is the best available use for the area, makes few demands on the fixed costs, and may provide added fertility for extractive enterprises that follow.

It is, however, largely because of a desire to understand more about the deployment of fixed costs that some farmers and managers have recently been seeking to develop enterprise accounts beyond the gross margin stage, towards the so-called 'net margin.' By allocating some of the lumpy and easily allocatable fixed costs, as well as the variable ones, net margins can be produced that can be helpful by:

1. Signalling the extent of the fixed costs.
2. Indicating why the fixed costs are being incurred and where they are being absorbed, leading to their more economic deployment.
3. Indicating how overall farm profit has been built up.
4. Providing the basis of the calculations that are required, if the elimination of a whole enterprise, as opposed to a marginal reduction or introduction expansion, is being contemplated.

In the difficult times which exist for farmers in the latter part of this century – when there is a need for fine tuning, when no stone must be left unturned in the search for profits, where diversification (often into non-farming enterprises) is being turned to, and when whole farming systems (including the use of set-aside) are being changed – these four issues increasingly occupy the minds of farmers and farm managers. In taking enterprise accounts beyond the gross margin stage and throwing light on those wider issues of farm planning, the logic of net margins is demonstrated in the diagram as shown in Fig. 9.4.

We see a strong possibility of more use in the future being made of net (as well as gross) margin calculations. Our reasons for saying this, underlying their four uses just listed, are as follows.

The first reason has already been mentioned but it bears repetition. The last decade and the middle and late 1970s in particular saw unprecedentedly large increases in the level of most fixed costs on many farms. Since then we have seen an era characterized by falling or static farm incomes which has led, through increased borrowing, to a significant increase in finance charges: in some cases of nagging, if not crippling, proportions. The dramatic increase in fixed costs has, alone, forced attention on to them. They simply can no longer be left on one side. The pressures that are currently being felt on product prices are leading, inevitably, to a search for lower-cost methods of farming and any search for cost reduction must

Fig. 9.4. A diagrammatic explanation of the contribution of several enterprises to total farm profit, expressing the analysis in terms of (a) gross margins and (b) net margins.

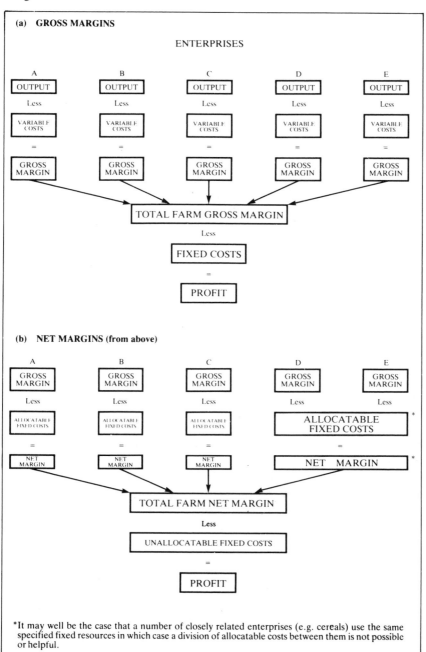

(a) GROSS MARGINS

ENTERPRISES

A	B	C	D	E
OUTPUT	OUTPUT	OUTPUT	OUTPUT	OUTPUT
Less	Less	Less	Less	Less
VARIABLE COSTS	VARIABLE COSTS	VARIABLE COSTS	VARIABLE COSTS	VARIABLE COSTS
=	=	=	=	=
GROSS MARGIN	GROSS MARGIN	GROSS MARGIN	GROSS MARGIN	GROSS MARGIN

TOTAL FARM GROSS MARGIN

Less

FIXED COSTS

=

PROFIT

(b) NET MARGINS (from above)

A	B	C	D	E
GROSS MARGIN	GROSS MARGIN	GROSS MARGIN	GROSS MARGIN	GROSS MARGIN
Less	Less	Less	Less	Less
ALLOCATABLE FIXED COSTS	ALLOCATABLE FIXED COSTS	ALLOCATABLE FIXED COSTS	ALLOCATABLE FIXED COSTS *	
=	=	=	=	
NET MARGIN	NET MARGIN	NET MARGIN	NET MARGIN *	

TOTAL FARM NET MARGIN

Less

UNALLOCATABLE FIXED COSTS

=

PROFIT

*It may well be the case that a number of closely related enterprises (e.g. cereals) use the same specified fixed resources in which case a division of allocatable costs between them is not possible or helpful.

automatically focus attention on the larger items of cost – invariably the 'fixed' ones.

Secondly, following directly from the 'magnitude factor', farmers increasingly want to understand more precisely exactly where and how their various fixed resources are being absorbed. This does not automatically imply a desire to alter radically the farming system; indeed in many instances that will not and perhaps cannot be the case. But attempts to reduce costs just because they are large may not get far without a detailed examination of how they are being employed and deployed on a day-to-day, week-to-week and season-to-season basis. In any situation, knowledge of what the facts are can often be the first real spur to action. The use of labour and machinery are especially important in this respect and a more effective use of either or both is more likely to follow with a detailed knowledge of what is happening than without it. That was the message of Work Study when it had its all too short heyday in British farming in the '50s and early '60s.

We do not advocate a timesheet mentality. Experience suggests that such detail can be too time-consuming, unlikely to be maintained in an industry not noted for its love of paperwork, and seldom, anyhow, put to sufficiently good use to justify its collection. The amount of detail that is recorded must be a matter for individuals depending upon their inclinations. But a reasonably accurate knowledge of how much labour is absorbed by each enterprise (and when) is likely to be sufficient in most cases for the degree of enterprise costing implied by the net margin approach. Time spent making it available will be time well spent. The same applies to machinery, and a critical consideration of the use of these two complementary inputs could be the first step to reducing (or employing more productively) these notoriously 'lumpy' and 'sticky' items of cost.

These examinations and quantifications will, anyhow, be an essential prerequisite to doing something constructive about the third reason for farmers' recent interest in fixed costs and net margins: namely to increase the understanding of how total farm profit has been built up. Since the 1960s gross margins helped to do this, but now they are leaving too much of the story unexplained. As the above diagram is intended to show, the allocation of the allocatable fixed costs (i.e. as far as the net margin) will take any understanding of how farm profit has been derived a lot further: as far, in fact, as it is probably necessary to go. It will be necessary for farm business economists and advisers to continue to warn farmers that trying to calculate the ultimate profit from each enterprise (unless there is only one) is an elusive, pointless and (worst of all) dangerous procedure. But it can never be good enough to stop at the gross margin. If total farm profit is important – and we all know how important it is – then the best possible understanding of how it has been derived must also be important. Net margins contribute to that understanding.

This leads to the fourth reason why this kind of approach is now wanted. The situation now confronting many British farmers is such that in addition to the fine tuning referred to earlier, they are also having to contemplate more radical remedies. This can involve introducing new enterprises as alternatives to or in addition to existing ones. Expanding existing ones may no longer be the answer. The new enterprises may be of several different kinds: conventional agricultural ones; new agricultural ones; what are being called the 'non-farming' enterprises, often of a value-adding kind directed at the food consumer or the leisure seeker; major new land based enterprises such as forestry, or activities quite unrelated to farming and land.

When brand new activities are being contemplated – or existing ones being dropped – it is much more than gross margins that are at stake. Once more, especially where mixed systems are involved, it will be the net margins that will be relevant. The partial budget all over again, if you like – but this time in the particular situation where an entire enterprise is being considered with all the costs that come or go with it. If, in the event, a particular enterprise is merely being reduced rather than eliminated, it is often the case that such a decision will have been reached after an initial consideration to eliminate it entirely. A knowledge of its net margin will have played its part in this thinking and will not have been wasted. Similarly if an enterprise is entirely displaced and some of its allocated costs do not leave the farm, but are put to alternative use, a complete knowledge of the inputs involved will, again, not have been wasted. In other words a knowledge of net margins may have been valuable in reaching a decision although what eventually happens may need to be tested by a partial budget which will seldom neatly coincide with the net margins themselves.

Our final point on this subject: although we believe that, properly interpreted, this kind of calculation is of value on a whole enterprise basis, it should not be expressed on a per hectare basis. That figure could only relate to the existing scale of the enterprise in question and would be misleading when contemplating subsequent marginal changes in scale. It is the very lumpiness of the fixed costs that results in them being spread more thinly or thickly over an enterprise according to its scale. Different answers would emerge with every variation in scale. It is the strength of the measure we term the gross margin that it does not behave in this way. That is what makes it so helpful as a means of exploring the likely effect of marginal changes. Nevertheless, we see an increasing interest in the net margin concept and, provided it stops short of trying to allocate items of cost that are not logically allocatable and provided it is interpreted carefully, we believe it will be relevant and helpful.

BUDGETS

This section concerns future trading and the preparation of budgets. There are four main kinds of budget which will be of most value in the management of a farm: complete budgets, partial budgets, break even and sensitivity budgets, and cash flows. The first two have already been touched upon, in the chapters on Control and Decision Making. They can, therefore, be dealt with briefly.

Complete budgets

In addition to providing a basis for budgetary control, complete budgets will be useful when:

1. A new farm is being tendered for or taken over.
2. When the system of farming on an existing farm is being so radically altered that a partial budget is inadequate to test the alternative systems.
3. Simply as an essential indicator at the beginning of each year, of the kind of profit that is likely to be obtained from the existing farming system.

In our experience, the greatest difficulty in preparing all budgets, of whatever kind, is not how to calculate them in the mechanical sense, but what figures to feed into them. As we have said before we have no answer to this problem other than as a colleague once said 'to muster all the accuracy that one possibly can'; to give careful consideration to the probabilities involved; not to disregard the value of reliable records about past performance on the farm in question; and to make the most careful estimate possible of likely prices and costs for the time period in question; all easier said than done. Clearly, to project too far forward is to trespass on the unknown. It is our belief, however, that farmers themselves are usually best placed to prepare their own budgets, and if an outsider is employed 'to hold their hand' it is still likely that the best place to prepare the budget is on the farm in question, along with the farmer, and with all the available data, not in an adviser's office miles away. There is, of course, plenty of assistance with the chore of budgeting these days, with computer programmes which enable a series of budgets to be prepared using different variables – or simply from the use of well laid out forms with all the appropriate headings of the kind supplied by the principal banks and others.

The layout and calculations required for a complete budget are shown below and a budget of this kind should be a routine management tool.

Inputs	Outputs

Purchased feed:
    productive units × quantity per unit
    × cost per unit
	Crops
	    productive units × yield per unit
	    × market price

Purchased seed:
    as for feed
	Milk
	    as for crops

Fertilizer: as for feed	

Rent and rates:
    actual level, allowing for possible
    increase
	Cattle ⎫ productive units × yield
	           ⎪ per unit × market price,
	           ⎪ (or, if more appropriate,
	 Sheep ⎬ value increase). Allow

Power and machinery:
    previous figures, appropriately
    adjusted, or separate estimates
    for each item involved
	⎪ for replacement stock by
	    ⎪ specifying sales (eg. culls
	 Pigs ⎪ and surplus young stock)
	    ⎪ and purchases, if
	    ⎪ replacements not home
	 Poultry ⎭ reared.

Labour:
    calculate person by person, allowing
    for increases, plus casual, etc.	

Other costs:
    previous figures, appropriately
    adjusted, or separate estimates
	Sundries
	    itemize and value

Profit	Loss
TOTAL	TOTAL

For an example of a complete budget the reader is referred back to the early part of our chapter on production when a budget was used to illustrate the financial quantification of a chosen farm system. Here we have concentrated on how to prepare a complete budget, item by item – and it is perhaps worth drawing attention to the different approaches to the calculation for the various kinds of item.

1. Variable inputs to productive units (purchased feed, seed and fertilizer) where the number of productive units, quantity per productive unit and price per unit of input are multiplied together:
    e.g. Conc. feed: 100×1.5 tonnes $\times$ £150 tonne = £22,500
2. Fixed inputs, where in the short term, actual figure is known e.g. rent.
3. Other input groupings (power and machinery, wages, sundries) where the previous global figure appropriately adjusted is used or where a cash item within grouping is calculated afresh (starting from zero if 'zero budgeting' is used – i.e. starting with a blank sheet and arguing the case for the inclusion of everything).

4. Output: number of productive units, yield per unit and price per unit of yield are multiplied together:

e.g. milk: 100×6000 litres $\times$ 20p litre $= £120,000$

with appropriate allowance for replacement stock.

5. Output where 'value increase' is the natural measure, e.g. livestock rearing

e.g. sale of £400 less purchase price of £100 = £300 output.

6. Sundry output – best itemized and valued separately especially if likely to vary between years.

Partial budgets

This is the financial management tool that farmers and managers are likely to require more than any other. The reason is simple. It is a method of assessing what any alert manager will be constantly thinking about; the possibility of advantageous change. Expansion, contraction, the introduction or discarding of activities, or a change in methods of production, can all be examined with the help of the partial budget. It embraces only those items of cost and return that will alter as a consequence of the contemplated change. When farmers talk of 'back of the envelope' calculations it is the partial budget approach that they are really talking of. Formally it takes the following form and answers the vital question, 'Is the total gain greater than the total loss?' The questions that have to be answered and the layout of the budget are as follows:

Gain	Loss
Extra revenue?	Lost revenue?
Avoided costs?	Extra costs?
Total (A)	Total (B)
Net gain = (A) – (B)	

The great value of this tool suggests that more should be written about it; in fact, its simplicity leaves relatively little to be added. It should be emphasized, however, that it cuts right across the concept of fixed and variable costs, taking account of any items that in any particular situation, will change. In some very simple situations, where for instance, two enterprises are being compared and where no change in fixed costs is envisaged a comparison of the gross margins, at whatever scale of change is involved, will in effect constitute the partial budget. More often than not, however, an orthodox partial budget will be required and will be safer – especially where the scale of the change is anything but very small. For example if the gross margin in £'s per hectare for two enterprises A and B is as follows then it follows that each hectare

	A	B
Output	600	700
Variable Costs	200	500
Gross Margin	400	200

changed from use B to A stand to add 200 (400−200) to the profit other things (e.g. fixed costs) remaining equal. The same question approached with a partial budget will give the same result, arrived at differently, as follows:

Gain		*Loss*	
£		£	
Extra revenue 600 (from A)		Lost revenue 700 (from B)	
Avoided costs 500 (from B)		Extra costs 200 (from A)	
Total 1100		900	

Net gain = £200 (1100 − 900)

It might therefore be argued that if a simple comparison of gross margins gives the same answer, why bother with a partial budget? The answer lies in the fact that our example concerned a switch of one hectare, while if it were two hectares, the gross margin would tell us (probably) correctly that the gain would be £400 (200 × 2). But would it give the correct answer if the switch involved 10 or 20 or 50 hectares? Probably not; other things, including previously fixed costs would begin to change and what would change would depend on the 'jumping off point' on the farm concerned i.e. which resources could accommodate the change, and which could not. The partial budget would invite us to question all items that might change – in the way that a simple comparison of two gross margins might not. It should do, but it just might not! That is why the partial budget has been referred to as the more 'wholesome' of the two approaches. Not that the use of partial budgets means that the user will automatically get it right. For while the methods of calculating individual items of input and output are similar to those used for complete budgeting, the difficulty remains (which is not so obviously a difficulty in complete budgeting) of identifying the items that will change. In complete budgeting, everything, by definition, is included. In some respects, therefore, partial budgets need more careful thinking about. But as in all things, practice makes perfect, and all farm managers should cultivate this particular practice. It is of real importance.

Break even budgets

This kind of budget can be useful where there is some doubt about the level of any particular variable, and the effect of possible variations in that level needs to be examined. This may be the case, especially, when a new enterprise is involved and there is nothing in the farm records to go on. The technique can be applied to either complete or partial budgeting situations. Important elements of yield or price can be varied to show the financial effect of different eventualities and, in particular, the minimum level of performance required to cover known costs. To take a very simple example, if on an all-arable farm, total costs are known to be £600 per hectare, and the expected price of cereals is £100 per tonne, then the break even yield will be 6 tonne per hectare (600 ÷ 100). How easily will that be obtained?

The technique could equally well be applied to inputs, but is more usually associated with outputs, which are usually less certain to predict. It is very much a trial and error approach, with one variable under the microscope at a time. In reality, of course, numerous variables will be influencing results at the same time. There may be a need, therefore, for a series of different budgets to test the effect of a whole range of possible price and yield levels in critical enterprises. This approach is known as sensitivity analysis – a practice that has much to commend it in times of uncertainty. It is similar to what is sometimes referred to as 'disaster budgeting' i.e. what will happen if this or that disaster happens? That does not aim to predict the break even position but (in similar manner) predicts the effect of a particular supposition. At all events there is a case for more than one budget: a conservative one, assuming the worst; a target one, aiming at the best; and for control purposes, a best possible estimate of what might actually happen. There is much to be learned from budgetary explorations of this kind. If a trading account answers the question, 'what has been done?', it is budgeting, that answers the more important forward-looking questions: 'what has to be done?', 'what should be done?', and 'what might be done?'.

Cash flows

A rather different kind of budget is the cash flow. It is not new to farming but it has been given new prominence in more recent years as inflation and increased uncertainty of prices and costs have given rise to new liquidity problems. A cash flow is merely a method of setting out actual cash outgoings and incomings over a period of time, indicating when each transaction is expected to occur, and what effect this will have on the cumulative balance: the bank balance or overdraft. A bank statement is, in fact, a kind of cash flow presented after the event.

The flow can be drawn up to suit the requirement of the individual or organisation concerned. It can relate to trading items only (although its purpose would then be very limited) or include also capital and personal expenditure, depending on whether the account contains both business and personal finances, or the two are kept separate. Non-cash item costs, such as depreciation, will not, of course, appear, although the purchase of new machines would be included as a capital item if and when it occurred. The cash flow can stretch as far ahead as is required (although after a couple of years it becomes increasingly speculative) and information can be set out in any required units of time, e.g. monthly, quarterly or annually. The balance can be struck for each time period, and a cumulative balance (beginning with the balance – overdraft existing at the commencement of the calculations) carried forward.

Over the years this kind of statement has been called a capital diary and a capital profile, but more recently it has been referred to universally as a cash flow.

Table 9.1. Framework for a cash flow.

Item	Time periods			
Receipts itemized	5,000 15,000	etc.	etc.	
Subtotal (1)	20,000	10,000	etc.	etc.
Expenses itemized	5,000 4,000 1,000	etc.		
Subtotal (2)	10,000	14,000	etc.	etc.
Balance for each time period (1)–(2) Cumulative balance	+10,000 +10,000*	−4,000 +6,000	etc. etc.	etc. etc.

*If zero at start.

The cash flow has a variety of uses, as follows:

---

1. For discounting future returns from investment projects (see ahead to 'investment appraisal')
2. For assessing the feasibility of investment projects, or simply the continuation of existing operations.
3. For knowing and being able to tell a lender the expected future level of a bank balance overdraft.
4. For simply forecasting the future pattern of events (i.e. the use of inputs, the receipt of outputs, the incidence of personal spending, including tax payment, planned investments, etc.)
5. As a means of adjusting the timing of payments and sales to the advantages of the business.
6. As a control check against which events can be monitored as they happen.

In (1) and (2) the entries would be limited to items related to the projects in question.

In the UK numerous advisory and commercial organizations, using computer facilities, offer cash flow and related services to the farming community. They are a valuable aid to management simply in charting the way forward. Bricks cannot be made without straw, however, and meaningful cash flow projections cannot be drawn up without first some orthodox annual complete budgets of the type already discussed in this and other chapters. The allocating forward of receipts and expenditure must be based on some assessment of what the total amount for the whole time period in question will be. Unlike the annual budget, however, the cash flow will depict a distinct 'shape', with peaks and troughs, which will reflect the nature of the farming system in question as well as something perhaps of the attitudes and trading habits of the farmer concerned.

Before leaving the subject of budgeting behind there is a final word to be said. Most discussion and writing about budgeting makes the basic assumption that, difficult as it may be, it is nevertheless possible to quantify all of the items involved. In fact, this is not the case, especially where fairly major investment projects are involved – as opposed to minor adjustments to existing systems – when some of the benefits that are being sought are in the form of improved technical performance and/or reduced physical and mental strain for operators and managers. A good example would be the introduction of a new milking parlour. Certain benefits of the kind just suggested will be hoped for but cannot be guaranteed, and even if they do in fact occur, it may be impossible to actually measure them. This problem is akin to those encountered on a much larger scale in major public investment projects, where recourse is made to cost-benefit methods. We do not suggest that farmers become involved in exercises of that magnitude but the fact remains that decisions which sometimes involve intangible items do have to be made. Despite the difficulties, systematic thinking is still likely to help. It will, therefore, always be sensible to proceed as far as possible with the appropriate budgets. If all of the credit items cannot be quantified at least a net cost can usually be arrived at against which the desired benefits can be weighed. Judgements of this kind will be very much better than nothing, if they only serve to identify where the break-even situation lies. We see farmers becoming more and more involved in decisions that involve not easily quantifiable issues as environmental and 'green' considerations become increasingly important, and social as well as economic arguments enter the equations.

BALANCE SHEETS

Structure and meaning of a balance sheet

If a trading account has some of the characteristics of a film, showing what is happening through time, then a balance sheet can be likened to a snapshot. It describes the financial state of a firm at a particular point of time. The trading account is more concerned with performance; the balance sheet with status. In principle, it is a straightforward enough document to understand, although in practice, the variations in layout and terminology that are employed by different accountants often create confusion. This no doubt has something to do with the fact that some farmers we have known have found considerable difficulties in interpreting their balance sheet; sometimes referring to their trading accounts and balance sheets jointly as 'the accounts' without clearly differentiating between the two.

It helps to have a simplified view of what to look for. Basically, all balance sheets show the total assets employed in a firm, and balance them against the liabilities. These two sets of information are usually set out side by side (but are sometimes presented in vertical form) and will look like this:

Liabilities	**Assets**
Current	Current
Long term	Fixed
Net worth	

In this sense, 'assets' simply means the capital employed whether it is very liquid (like cash in hand) or very fixed (like land). The most usual farming balance sheet convention is to list assets in ascending order of liquidity, with cash at the top and land at the bottom – although we sometimes see it the other way around. It is usually subdivided into the current assets, at the top, including such items as cash in hand, bank balances, debts owed to the business, stores on hand and trading livestock, followed by fixed assets including breeding livestock, machinery and equipment, land and buildings. In many ways this is a rather arbitrary division of things, but it conveniently describes the situation.

Since, in an accounting sense, businesses are deemed to have an existence of their own, all of these assets must have been financed by somebody and ultimately – and certainly should the business for any reason be wound up – owners of capital will want it returned. To the extent that the proprietor himself is an owner of some of this capital, he takes his place amongst the others to whom the business has a 'liability'. This allows all of the assets to be balanced equally against all of the liabilities. The assets describe how the capital is deployed; the liabilities describe who owns it. Like the assets, the liabilities are conventionally arranged in ascending order of liquidity and are also divided into current and longer term items. The former consists of such items as any debts owing by the farm, overdraft, tax debts, etc., and the latter of longer term private loans and fixed term loans such as mortgages. Hopefully, assets will exceed the liabilities to outsiders, and the proprietor will then own the balance. This amount is known as the net worth. It is the owner's stake in his own business, and is also known as the equity capital. If it is positive, the firm is solvent, which means that if it is sold out, realizing all of its capital, all liabilities could be met, with something left over. If liabilities to others exceed the assets, the reverse would be true, with all that that implies.

That is the essence of the balance sheet. Any balance sheet (no matter how complicated it looks) should be read with that simple conceptual framework in mind. Any more complicated view of it is probably unhelpful. A 'typical' tenanted farm business balance sheet might for instance in round figures look like the one in Table 9.2.

Balance sheet ratios

In recent years, in the UK at least, it has been fashionable to look for ways in which balance sheet ratios may be calculated and used. It is undoubtedly true that like the trading account, the balance sheet has important messages to offer. Certainly, managers should be able to recognize and interpret the appropriate messages, but to calculate too many apparently precise measures and base decisions too closely on them is difficult, if not

Table 9.2. A tenant farm balance sheet.

Liabilities	£	£	Assets	£	£
Current			**Current**		
Creditors	5,000		Cash in hand	500	
Bank overdraft	20,000		Debtors	4,500	
			Stores	10,000	
Fixed			Tillages	5,000	
			Non-breeding		
Loan	25,000		Livestock	30,000	
Subtotal		50,000	Subtotal		50,000
			Fixed		
			Breeding		
			livestock	50,000	
New worth			Machinery		
(i.e. owner's stake)		200,000	and equipment	150,000	
					200,000
Total		250,000	Total		250,000

mistaken. Pressure to become involved in this area of management may have been placed upon the farming community by the ancillary and consultancy brigades. The measures are there and have a professional ring to them so they should be used! Fortunately, there is a healthy safeguard in that most farmers learn to become good judges of what is useful to them – and what is not – and not only in this area of management. We have yet to meet the farmer who indulges in sophisticated balance sheet calculations, although no doubt there are a few who do and who get some benefit from them. Despite its age, one of the best guides to this subject that we know is the article, listed in Further Reading, by Ian Reid. He discusses the meaning of the messages rather than the arithmetic. Important amongst the messages are:

1. the need for a healthy net worth (many bankers like to see an owner having about a 50% stake in his own business);
2. the riskiness of a 'high gearing' situation in which net worth is allowed to be too low and high borrowing charges have a first and heavy call on profits;
3. the need to maintain a healthy balance between current assets and current liabilities so that any call to repay short-term borrowing (including overdrafts) can be met without recourse to disposing of non-liquid assets – a situation known as 'overtrading';

4. the importance of flexibility that comes from a healthy degree of liquidity or potential liquidity; and
5. the importance of maintaining a sensible balance between current and fixed assets.

Too much capital in fixed assets without the working capital to farm them will produce a sterile situation. Reid uses the analogy of an over-bodied car that will be easily overtaken by its competitors on the road. His article deserves reading. So, more recently, does the relevant chapter in Warren's book and the little non-farming book by Proctor mentioned in the Further Reading.

Apart from the matter of return on capital – which we turn to next – we doubt if there is more that most farmers-managers need to extract from their balance sheets nor even, perhaps, whether they actually need to calculate ratios as such. We do not know many bank managers who cover their desks with balance sheet ratios (beyond the relative size of net worth) when farmers approach them for loans. They lend to farmers not farms! An ability, however, to recognize the various absolute amounts that have been discussed here will count for a lot. Some of the ratios, in fact, will become self-evident from that inspection. We conclude that it is certainly important for a manager to have a good understanding of balance sheet layout, to appreciate a limited number of relationships within it, and to be able to recognize trends over time. A great deal in all this will depend, however, on the competence of the individual, on how others see him or her and on his or her own attitudes to risk.

Return on existing capital

We have included a discussion of this topic here, rather than under investment appraisal, because it is concerned with obtained results, not with an assessment of future investment. It links the profit and loss account with the balance sheet and it seemed appropriate, therefore, to deal with it here.

Since the balance sheet tells us how much and what kind of capital is invested in a business, it is natural to look to it when we wish to relate the profit, as depicted in the profit and loss account, to the amount of capital that was required to generate it. In doing so, however, two important points must be remembered. First, that a balance sheet is struck once a year and therefore represents a measure of the capital employed only at that point of time. A more accurate measure would need to take account of the fluctuations, particularly in working capital, employed throughout the year. That can be done with the help of cash flow calculations, but it is time-consuming and research work into this area has indicated that the errors involved in simply taking the average of beginning and year-end figures are not usually great. Secondly, the asset figures in any balance sheet are as accurate as the valuations employed. If, as is often the case with long term assets, they have remained unadjusted while asset values have in fact increased, they will clearly be inaccurate. These days, also, the value of intangible assets such as the value of a milk quota is part of the asset array. The true capital actually invested in a business at any point of time is the capital that could be taken out at the same point of time and reinvested elsewhere.

The thought of doing just that may be one of several reasons why a farmer wishes to calculate the current return on his existing capital. These reasons include a desire to compare this calculation with:

1. Standard figures for similar businesses.
2. The corresponding figures in the business in question in previous years.
3. The prediction (if it exists) for the year in question.
4. Comparable figures in other industries and investment outlets which might provide alternatives.

Several different kinds of calculations can be made depending on the ownership circumstances and questions to be answered. So care must be taken when comparing like with like. Three of them will be mentioned here.

First, there is return on the tenant-type capital, reflecting the result of farming the land as opposed to owning. It is calculated as follows:

$$\frac{\text{Profit (management and investment income)}^* \times 100}{\text{all capital except land and buildings}}$$

The magnitude of this figure will clearly vary according to the potential of the farming system involved and the capability of the individual. In post-war years, in the UK, the figure for many orthodox farming systems has on average ranged between 15% and 20%. It should be remembered, however, that the profit figure used here conventionally includes a return to management as well as to capital – and recently (we are writing in 1990) returns have been much lower, often well down into single figures.

Secondly, of more interest to the owner occupier, there is return on all the assets employed, including the land, i.e.:

$$\frac{\text{profit (without any charge for rent)} \times 100}{\text{all capital (tenant's and landlord's)}}$$

*The management and investment income is the residual after a charge has been made for unpaid manual labour but before a charge has been made for capital or management.

The average level of this calculation is inherently much lower than that for tenant-type capital, and is frequently down in the low single figures.

A third and important measure, that will be of interest to all farmers (tenants or owner occupiers) who include borrowed money amongst their liabilities, is the net return, after borrowing charges, accruing to their own share of the capital. This time the calculation, which will reflect particularly the financing arrangements of any individual farm business, will be:

$$\frac{\text{profit less interest on borrowed capital} \times 100}{\text{total capital employed less borrowed capital}}$$

All three measures have three things in common. First, caution should be exercised in placing too much reliance on the absolute accuracy of any such calculations. Warnings have already been sounded about the inexactitude of profit calculations and of asset valuation. It should be remembered, therefore, that calculations of return on capital may compound any errors. Secondly, these rates of return are concerned with past results, and by themselves offer no insight into the performance levels that have brought those results about. They are of historical interest, but even when low by 'opportunity cost' standards they do not in our experience lead to a situation in which individuals, well bedded into the farming industry, jump to the conclusion that they should be doing something else with their capital and labour. Thirdly, they have a limited value when it comes to directing the future deployment of capital. That is, in many ways, a more interesting and important topic, and is the subject of the final section of this chapter.

INVESTMENT APPRAISAL

The importance of fresh investment

For some time now farmers have been complaining that they have to 'pedal' faster and faster in order to stay where they are. Translated into financial terms, they have had to intensify and to invest more and more in order to maintain existing profit margins. It is hardly surprising, therefore, that we have seen an increasing awareness in farming circles of capital and cash problems, and that investment has featured strongly in recent farm management literature – just as comparative analysis, budgeting and, finally, gross margins did during the 1950s, early 1960s and 1970s respectively.

To the extent, however, that existing investment represents a past commitment and is very often irrevocable, the element of agricultural capital that should come under the closest scrutiny is that small share of it that is being freshly invested and remains uncommitted until it has actually been invested. In theory, even past investment is constantly being freshly invested in the sense that if it is decided to leave it where it is, it is, in effect, being 'reinvested' in its present use. Also, some farmers do make positive provisions for reinvestment, occasionally making major alterations to their farming systems, and, therefore, to their patterns of investment. A large proportion of farm capital, however, tends to remain more or less where it is and 'good management' provides the best assurance that an adequate return accrues to it.

Appraisal methods

This situation makes it all the more important that whenever an opportunity presents itself to make a considered decision about whether or not to invest in a particular way, the opportunity should not be neglected. In practice, farmers and farm managers confront this opportunity in a variety of ways. In our experience, it is only occasionally that formal investment appraisal techniques are applied. Despite the recent interest in these techniques it remains a fact that the more sophisticated of them (e.g. net present value and internal rate of return methods) are very infrequently used, and even the more simple methods – 'pay-back' and 'return on outlay' – only occasionally so. This is a pity. Application of the last two appraisal methods referred to is not complicated and even if applied in a rough and ready way would add some degree of worthwhile objectivity to the more intuitive approach. The return on outlay method simply relates additional profit expected from an investment, calculated as in a partial budget, to the extra capital required, i.e.:

$$\text{Return on outlay} = \frac{\text{Extra profit} \times 100}{\text{extra capital}} \text{ say } \frac{£2,000 \times 100}{£10,000} = 20\%$$

Admittedly the extra capital may not be as easy to calculate in net terms as the extra profit, especially where there is an offsetting effect on the new capital required from old capital that might be released. Sometimes it is suggested that the return should be calculated on half of the new investment on the assumption that, because of depreciation, any investment will vary from its initial value to zero. This, however, overlooks the fact that the initial amount has to be found and that, in theory at least, a depreciation fund should be used (which can itself be invested) to keep the investment intact.

The pay-back method of assessment is equally straightforward. It simply involves dividing expected profit (before any charge for depreciation has been made) into the investment required, and measures how many years it will take to recoup that investment, i.e.:

$$\text{Pay-back} = \frac{\text{total extra investment}}{\text{extra annual profit}} \quad \text{say} \quad \frac{£10,000}{£2,500} = 4$$
$$\text{years}$$

(without a charge for depreciation)

It will be noticed that this method provides an appraisal expressed in time, compared with the percentage answer provided by the return on outlay method and it is therefore (unlike 'return on outlay') not an assessment of worthwhileness. It is, rather, an indication of uncertainty (akin to sensitivity analysis) for the longer the pay-back period the less certainty there can be of knowing what the pay-back will actually be.

Both of these appraisal methods (return on outlay and pay-back) while very much better than nothing, are fairly crude compared with those methods based on discounting – recognizing the 'time value' of money – and therefore have considerable advantages when major projects are involved which are expected to yield a return over an extended time period with unequal returns between the years. Such techniques take account of the fact that because of the interest earning capacity of capital, funds earned today are worth more than a similar quantity return tomorrow. To take account of this fact, discounting tables or formulae can be applied to future returns in order to equate them with present day values. This is the reverse of compounding. Present sums can be compounded forward (at a chosen rate of interest) to give their enhanced value at any given time in the future. Correspondingly, future amounts of money (accruing to an investment now) can be discounted to give their present value. This discounting process is in essence the basis of both the Net Present Value and the Internal Rate of Return methods of investment appraisal. In the case of the former, future net cash flows over the projected life of the investment (including any terminal value) are discounted to their present value and compared with the present value of the investment (i.e. in year 0) showing the extent of gain (or loss). By way of simple example the calculations will look like those shown in Table 9.3.

The Internal Rate of Return method differs from the NPV in that, by trial and error, that value of interest is found which when used to discount future cash flows exactly equates their present value with the value of the initial investment. It measures the rate of interest that can be afforded for the investment capital for the project break even. Any borrowing rate below this level indicates profit. This time the arithmetic looks like the example in Table 9.4.

Table 9.3. Net Present Value method of investment appraisal.

Time period	Net cash flow (£k)	Discount (10%)	Discounted net cash flow
0 (initial outlay)	10	Discount factor	0.0
Year 1	7	0.909	6.4
Year 2	5	0.826	4.1
Year 3	3	0.751	2.3
Year 4	3	0.683	2.1
			14.9

In this example, with initial capital costed for simplicity at 10%, £10,000 is invested and yields net returns, over 4 years, of, £7,000, £5,000, £3,000, and £3,000, respectively. The total Present Value of those returns is £14,900, giving a positive benefit compared with the initial outlay (£10,000), of £4,900. This is the Net Present Value.

Table 9.4. Internal Rate of Return method of investment appraisal.

Time period	Net cash flow (£k)	Discount 40%	Discounted net cash flow
0 (initial outlay)	10	Discount factor	0.0
Year 1	7	0.714	5.0
Year 2	5	0.510	5.0
Year 3	3	0.364	1.1
Year 4	3	0.260	0.8
			9.5

Here the discount rate which, when applied to the net cash flows over the four year life of the investment most nearly equates their combined present value (£9,500) with the cost of the initial outlay (£10,000), is 40%. This is the price that can be paid for the capital, for the investment to break even. In this case there appears to be some margin to spare — but a cautionary note must always be sounded.

It is our experience that the concepts underlying these 'discounted' techniques are not easily assimilated. There comes a time, however, when the penny drops. One of the problems, of course, is that familiarity with the methods only comes with practice and it is perhaps only cost accountants and investment analysts who actually use such techniques frequently. Those who wish to remedy that situation should consult Warren or one of the other farm management texts we have recommended. We have included in Table 9.5 the discounting tables that will be required; we wish you many happy returns!

Table 9.5. Discount factors for calculating the present value of future cash flows.

Interest rate	Years									
	1	2	3	4	5	6	7	8	9	10
1%	0.9901	0.9803	0.9706	0.9610	0.9515	0.9420	0.9327	0.9235	0.9143	0.9053
2%	0.9804	0.9612	0.9423	0.9238	0.9057	0.8880	0.8706	0.8535	0.8368	0.8203
3%	0.9709	0.9426	0.9151	0.8885	0.8626	0.8375	0.8131	0.7894	0.7664	0.7441
4%	0.9615	0.9246	0.8890	0.8548	0.8219	0.7903	0.7599	0.7307	0.7026	0.6756
5%	0.9524	0.9070	0.8638	0.8227	0.7835	0.7462	0.7107	0.6768	0.6446	0.6139
6%	0.9434	0.8900	0.8396	0.7921	0.7473	0.7050	0.6651	0.6274	0.5919	0.5584
7%	0.9436	0.8734	0.8163	0.7629	0.7130	0.6663	0.6227	0.5820	0.5439	0.5083
8%	0.9259	0.8573	0.7938	0.7350	0.6806	0.6302	0.5835	0.5403	0.5002	0.4632
9%	0.9174	0.8417	0.7722	0.7084	0.6499	0.5963	0.5470	0.5019	0.4604	0.4224
10%	0.9091	0.8264	0.7513	0.6830	0.6209	0.5645	0.5132	0.4665	0.4241	0.3855
11%	0.9009	0.8116	0.7312	0.6587	0.5935	0.5346	0.4817	0.4339	0.3909	0.3522
12%	0.8929	0.7972	0.7118	0.6355	0.5674	0.5066	0.4523	0.4039	0.3606	0.3220
13%	0.8850	0.7831	0.6931	0.6133	0.5428	0.4803	0.4251	0.3762	0.3329	0.2946
14%	0.8772	0.7695	0.6750	0.5921	0.5194	0.4556	0.3996	0.3506	0.3075	0.2679
15%	0.8696	0.7561	0.6575	0.5718	0.4972	0.4323	0.3759	0.3269	0.2843	0.2472
16%	0.8621	0.7432	0.6407	0.5523	0.4761	0.4104	0.3538	0.3050	0.2630	0.2267
17%	0.8547	0.7305	0.6244	0.5337	0.4561	0.3898	0.3332	0.2848	0.2434	0.2080
18%	0.8457	0.7182	0.6086	0.5158	0.4371	0.3704	0.3139	0.2660	0.2255	0.1911
19%	0.8403	0.7062	0.5934	0.4987	0.4190	0.3521	0.2959	0.2487	0.2090	0.1756
20%	0.8333	0.6944	0.5787	0.4823	0.4019	0.3349	0.2791	0.2326	0.1938	0.1615
25%	0.8000	0.6400	0.5120	0.4096	0.3277	0.2621	0.2097	0.1678	0.1342	0.1074
30%	0.7692	0.5917	0.4552	0.3501	0.2693	0.2072	0.1594	0.1226	0.0943	0.0725
35%	0.7407	0.5487	0.4064	0.3011	0.2230	0.1652	0.1224	0.0906	0.0671	0.0497
40%	0.7143	0.5102	0.3644	0.2603	0.1859	0.1328	0.0949	0.0678	0.0484	0.0346
45%	0.6897	0.4756	0.3280	0.2262	0.1560	0.1076	0.0742	0.0512	0.0353	0.0243
50%	0.6667	0.4444	0.2963	0.1975	0.1317	0.0878	0.0585	0.0390	0.0260	0.0173

It should not be supposed that, because of the apparent sophistication of these two techniques, they will, automatically, produce black and white answers that can be relied upon in all circumstances, leaving the manager with no decisions to take, no judgement to exercise, no gut feelings to call upon. The techniques remain vulnerable, like any budgetary techniques, to attempts to project anticipated costs and returns too far ahead. As we have implied, such methods, though not as complicated as they sometimes appear, are not yet often used by farmers and that situation may well continue. More often than not, investors are inclined to follow a particular line because instinctively they believe it to be right or simply because they want to do it. These largely intuitive reasons for investing can be perfectly sound ones, especially if they are influenced by past investment which (with a due regard for future possible price and cost trends) has proved to be sound. We have sympathy with the well known and respected farmer who when asked about his investment appraisal techniques, thought for a while and then said 'They are in my stomach, not my head!'. By themselves, however, it cannot be denied that intuitive approaches do lack the objectivity of some more formal investment appraisal and must always be suspect for this reason. But equally, the formal techniques rely upon a degree of knowledge about internal and external factors which sometimes calls their reliance into question.

This seems an unsatisfactory state of affairs in which to leave this subject. Investment decisions do have to be made, and made now in anticipation of future returns. In the belief that some form of systematic, unpretentious, but palatable kind of appraisal could help to provide a safeguard against the inadvertent misuse of capital, we offer the following checklist as a kind of investor's safety net.

INVESTMENT CHECKLIST

1. First and foremost, have you looked for ways of improving income without using extra capital at all? There may be – indeed usually are – opportunities for tightening up on management or adjusting existing systems of farming which may even release capital. These opportunities should be fully explored before more capital is pumped in. In the majority of cases, and if properly interpreted, the established methods of farm business analysis (of the kind discussed earlier in this chapter) will provide an adequate guide here. If, however, fresh investment really is required, or you are simply seeking an outlet on the farm for available funds, then:

2. Have you budgeted for the change? This should always be done, using a partial budget. Weigh the extra returns and avoided costs against the extra costs and lost returns. If possible relate the answer to the extra capital involved. Ignore things that will not change.

3. Are you giving priority to those enterprises from which you can be reasonably certain of a measurable return? Or are you just hoping, in some vague way, that things will be better?

4. Are you about to expand a job that you know you are doing well? This usually means knowing the gross margins for your various enterprises. And what about the relative future prospects for each of them?

5. If you are about to commit yourself to a new venture, have you made sure that you have the true facts about it? Or have you relied on hearsay or vague reporting?

6. How long will you have to wait for your return? Investment always means outlay now for a return some time in the future. The further ahead that future is, the more uncertain any forecast of the return will be. Other things being equal, a return sooner is preferable to a return later.

7. If necessary, can your investment be liquidated and reinvested in another form? A certain amount of investment in fixed equipment will always be necessary, but the ability to transfer capital from one enterprise to another may be a valuable tactic, especially for the younger farmer, who usually needs capital but often finds it hard to borrow.

8. Will the new investment actually generate income? Livestock and crops, by their very nature, do this. Other types of investment (e.g. buildings, roads, machinery), necessary as they may be, merely assist. By themselves they generate nothing except costs. A reasonable balance between the two types of capital must be maintained, but always with sufficient of the income-generating kind.

9. Are you carrying out your investment in the cheapest possible way, consistent with your own technical standards? There are two aspects of cheapness: the interest you will pay on borrowed capital, and the amount of capital that is actually employed. It is easy to pay too much attention to the former and not enough to the latter. The question to ask is, 'how little capital do I need?' not, 'how much?'. A well conceived and presented plan in these terms will help to convince a lender that you have a good case.

10. Finally, if you are investing on labour saving grounds, where is the saving? Is your wages bill actually being reduced, or is there to be some additional output as a result of labour being released? Sometimes, especially where competition for labour is strong, it may be necessary to invest simply in order to keep the labour you have. But where so-called labour saving is the motive, be quite clear in your own mind about what this really means to the farm economy.

These ten points were once referred to as our Ten Commandments! We prefer to regard them as the ten questions which make up our own informal approach to investment appraisal. The genuine feeling, after answering the questions, that an investment proposition 'feels right' may be worth more than all of the investment appraisal techniques put together!

Let us conclude by reflecting on an earlier thought: namely that the use of capital is in many respects what farming is all about. Many investment decisions centre around the word 'choice'. The choice between different investment possibilities on many farms is endless, as is the range in the returns that these investments can offer. Well conceived, marginal investments on existing and well managed farms can provide very good returns indeed; ill conceived, the return can be nil. Where no formal appraisal of an investment is being undertaken – and this may often be the case – the use of a checklist of the sort offered here may help. Few investments score on every front – but if you can satisfy yourself on seven or eight of our ten points that may provide some assurance that the investment is well conceived. So next time you are contemplating a fresh investment, have a good look at this checklist, especially question one!

OUR FINAL THOUGHT

It may help a prospective borrower to prepare his case if he thinks himself

into the position of the prospective lender. All of the questions that will be
asked will become obvious.

QUESTIONS AND EXERCISES

- Using your latest profit and loss account, making the necessary
  adjustments and introducing any necessary additional
  information
  - recast the data into a statement of inputs and outputs and
  - with the help of published standards, carry out a systematic
    examination of the data with a view to improving efficiency.

- Calculate the net margin for each of your main enterprises.

- - Prepare a complete budget for your present farm system for the
    coming financial year.
  - Prepare a partial budget for at least one change to the system
    that you are contemplating.

- Inspect your balance sheet and check it against the five
  'messages' (balance sheet ratios) discussed in this chapter.

- Using the latest available figures calculate the return on your
  existing capital (using the one of the three calculations shown
  which is appropriate to your circumstances and/or needs).

- For the next investment you are contemplating
  - apply any of the appraisal techniques discussed in this chapter
  - apply the 10 point checklist suggested here.

A GUIDE TO FURTHER READING

Giles, A. K. (1986) *Net margins and all that – an essay in management accounting in
agriculture.* University of Reading, Farm Management Unit, Study No. 9.
  An account of the history of farm management accounting in agriculture in
  the UK leading up to the recent interest in net margins.

Norman, L., Turner, R. and Wilson, K. (1985) *The Farm Business.* Longman, London.
  Chapter 5 contains helpful examples of the arithmetic of investment appraisal.

Proctor, R. (1986) *Finance for the Perplexed Executive.* Fontana, London.
  A priceless read – don't miss it.

Reid, I. G. (1969) Balance Sheet Interpretation. *Farm Management* 1, (6) 8–14.
  Still the best and most readable assessment of the subject that we know.

Sturrock, F. G. (1971) *Farm Accounting and Management.* Pitman, London.
The best book that we know on the accounting and book-keeping aspects of farm management.

Warren, M. F. (1986) *Financial Management for Farmers.* Hutchinson Education, London. Chapter 4 especially and the book generally expand on what we have tried to cover in a few pages.

Chapter 10

Staff

Qualitative and quantitative importance
Staff planning
Recruitment
Training
Motivation
Leadership
Reducing staff
Positive and negative contributions to efficient staffing

QUALITATIVE AND QUANTITATIVE IMPORTANCE

This chapter concerns the farm staff, the resource which holds the key to productivity. It is well known that labour is important as a quantitative element in the cost of production. What is less obviously appreciated is the qualitative influence of staff on the efficient use of all other resources.

A notable feature of the farming industry in many countries, especially in the developed world, has been the continued reduction in the size of the workforce, with increased mechanization and a corresponding increase in labour productivity. Heavy manual chores remain a feature of work on some smaller farms but the tendency is to expect the majority of workers to be equipped with a wider range and higher level of skills. There is an enormous range in the working conditions from one holding to another, but on the whole, farm work offers both interest and satisfaction. The work, except in certain types of intensive enterprise, is varied by season, by day and even within the hour. Of considerable significance is the fact that at the completion of a work period, staff can usually see clearly what has been achieved. It may well be that a field has been cleared of bales or a group of animals has been vaccinated – in the latter case evidenced by empty bottles. Some jobs can be so repetitive as to be monotonous and others unpleasant and dirty, but the increasing availability of equipment, such as improved

155

safety cabs and air-flow helmets, are helping to make the farm a safer, cleaner and healthier place to work.

The generally good labour relations that exist in agriculture are a feature of the industry in which it can take pride and one which must be maintained and developed. It is aided by the relatively small numbers of people involved and by the close personal contact that most employees have with the boss. Communications can then be direct, objectives and plans discussed and agreed. In most cases staff obtain satisfaction from a close involvement in the operation of a business. With the development of larger scale farming businesses, however, there is the need for a more formal approach to the structure of the organization, and in these circumstances there is a considerable challenge to management to provide the necessary motivation in each section of the business. The unity that pervades the small farm can easily be lost.

Compared to the situation in the manufacturing industries, much less research has been undertaken into the factors which influence the performance of farm staff, but the classical work of Herzberg, who identified 'satisfiers' and 'dissatisfiers', is particularly relevant to the farm scene.

Before employees can begin to take real pride in their work, any dissatisfiers, such as low wage levels, inadequate housing or poor working conditions, need to be remedied. Managers can then give full consideration to the satisfiers, such as delegation of responsibilities, which lead to improved job satisfaction and labour productivity.

It is against this background that we will examine a number of particular aspects of this part of management, which managers need to consider in order to create the optimum environment. We begin with the important topic of staff planning.

STAFF PLANNING

Many farms operate, at any given point of time, with the labour force which they happen to have acquired over a period, and factors other than a genuine present economic need will have influenced this situation. The supply of labour, therefore, may or may not match the real present need of the farm. An objective and continuing assessment of labour requirements and availability should therefore be made both for the present and with a watchful eye on the future.

Techniques of varying sophistication are available for use in staff planning, according to the scale of the business, but in all situations the thought processes should be the same. The essence of staff planning is that after overall objectives have been established, a clear endeavour is made:

1. to ensure optimum use of human resources currently employed, and

?. to plan for future staff needs in terms of such aspects as skills, numbers, age and experience.

The planning process should result in the employment of the correct number of staff, with the necessary talents and skills, doing the appropriate job, performing the right activity and above all working towards the achievement of objectives.

These ends are achieved by defining objectives for the long and short terms, by arranging activities to be carried out using the best methods and by defining the various jobs. Appropriate recruiting and training, as detailed below, can then take place to correct any weaknesses in the existing staff.

Assessing the number of workers required to run a farm can be done, especially for small enterprises, without too much fuss by experienced judgements. In the more complex situation however, where some calculation is required, it is best done by using the 'standard man days' approach. This is a rather simple technique and is by no means perfect. It involves multiplying the hectares of each crop and the headage of each different livestock type by a known 'standard man day' figure (i.e. 8 hours). It is usual to add 15% to the total to allow for maintenance work, and the results need to be interpreted in the light of such factors as the type and layout of livestock buildings, the availability and capacity of machinery, the soil type, and especially, the seasonal variation of labour requirement with crops.

An example of the requirements for an arable and sheep farm is shown in Table 10.1. Here, the ideal staffing would be one full time shepherd, one tractor driver/relief shepherd, one full time tractor driver, the farmer and casual labour for lambing and harvest.

A labour profile can also be prepared to illustrate seasonal peaks and

Table 10.1. Standard man day (SMD) calculation of labour requirements.

400 ha farm	SMDs per unit	Total SMDs
800 ewes	× 0.5	400
80 ha grazing	× 1.0	80
200 ha winter wheat (straw baled)	× 2.25	80
120 ha spring barley (straw baled)	× 2.25	270
Total		1200
Plus 15% for maintenance		180
Total labour requirement		1380
1380 ÷ 300 (number of working days in the year) = 4.6 people		

troughs. It should not be interpreted too literally but used as a guide to indicate problem periods. Consideration can be given to minimizing peak requirements by improved mechanization, change of variety or modific-ations to the cropping programme. The use of casual labour and contract services and improvement of gang organization can also be considered. Peak requirements can often be dealt with in the small farm by inputs of family labour, and in larger organizations by diverting staff who are at other times largely involved in maintenance duties. Having employees with a wide range of skills and a flexible attitude shown by their willingness to move from job to job is a considerable asset to any business.

The seasonal requirements of the same arable and sheep farm is shown on a labour profile in Table 10.2. The same profile is illustrated diagram-matically in Fig. 10.1.

Table 10.2. Labour profile (man hours per month).

	J	F	M	A	M	J	Jly	A	S	O	N	D	Total
Sheep	240	240	800	320	240	320	160	160	280	200	160	160	3280
Winter wheat	0	0	150	330	90	90	500	900	800	850	180	0	3890
Spring barley	0	0	600	100	180	0	0	650	300	100	150	100	2180
													9350

The example indicates that in the months of March, August, September and October the normal hours provided by the four regular staff do not meet the needs of the system.

Some possible solutions are therefore:

1. use overtime especially in October
2. lamb the ewe flock in February
3. if lambing in March, aim to plant spring cereal in February
4. employ casual help with lambing and harvest
5. employ a contractor to bale and cart the straw
6. undertake maintenance December to February
7. arrange holidays in May, June and early July.

RECRUITMENT

Having considered the need to match the skills and abilities of staff to the needs of the jobs to be done we turn to recruitment. The opportunity to recruit a new member of staff is a most important occasion and one justi-fying considerable management input. On many farms it is an infrequent

Fig. 10.1. Labour profile for a sheep and arable farm.

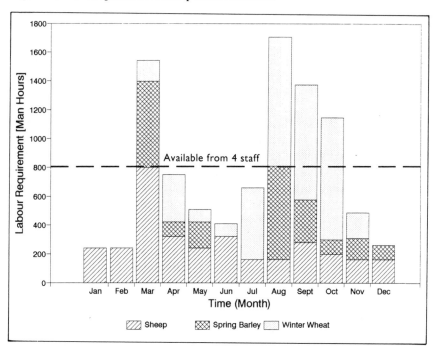

event, so that many managers get inadequate experience to become suitably skilled in this important function. Guidance can be obtained from published material including that which is listed at the end of this chapter, and recruitment is an essential part of the syllabus of training courses in staff management. it may well be advisable, in the case of a senior appointment or in the early years of a manager's career, to employ professional assistance.

The recruitment process can be divided into four parts.

The job and person required

Before replacing a member of staff or appointing an additional person, it is necessary to consider the situation in detail and to decide if there is, in fact, a worthwhile vacancy. With increased mechanization, and the re-organizing of duties, it may be that recruitment is unjustified. Some re-organization may be essential if the person has left the farm because he or she found the job too difficult, too boring, or providing insufficient challenge. Knowing that there is a post to be filled, it is then of considerable value to the manager and to potential employees for details of the job to be written down, i.e. for a job description to be prepared. This will include essential aspects such as working hours, pay, holiday arrangements, housing and prerequisites, as well as the responsibilities and associated authorities. It should also outline any particular difficulties and cover such items as the opportunities for training or development. It is a document that will be retained by the person appointed and a periodic check through the office copy is a worthwhile exercise for the employer.

After describing the job, a full description of the ideal person to fill the vacancy should follow. Applicants receiving such a document will be able to judge for themselves whether they wish to be considered further. the details will include age, family, health, experience, qualifications and skills. Intelligence, disposition and interests will be of importance, especially if the person is to take a post with responsibility of work in a team with existing staff. A suitable person may be available in the business but if not the next stage follows.

Obtaining suitable candidates

For a proportion of vacancies, advertising in the local or national press will be unnecessary, but for others, and especially the most important jobs, the cost of advertising will be well justified. Some farmers, for instance, report better response by advertising for stockmen in the local papers of grassland areas of the west and north of Britain or for tractor drivers in the arable east. The advertisement needs to be attractive, clearly worded, without unnecessary detail, but with explicit application procedure. A well-prepared application form is helpful in most instances, although for manual jobs it can be off-putting to potential applicants. The facility to make reversed charges calls in the evening is probably more appropriate here.

Selection

A difficult task now follows in assessing the information received from applicants and in selecting the ones to be invited for interview. Being able to contact applicants by telephone is beneficial especially when making interview arrangements, but also for checking queries, finding out why they want to move, and at the same time gaining useful first impressions as to their general approach and personality. If it is possible, a visit to see the applicant in his present job, to meet his family and perhaps see how they care for the cottage, is a very advantageous practice. The interview itself is a most important event requiring adequate preparation and should be used primarily to judge how well each candidate would be likely to fit the job, but also for them to decide, after full discussions, whether they want the job. Time is usually a precious commodity when recruiting, as the person being replaced has probably already left the farm and the duties are being performed by other staff members or perhaps by the farmer himself. Nevertheless, interviews should not be rushed and time should be allocated to showing applicants the farm and the housing, explaining the location of shops and schools, and introducing them to other members of staff. Complications can arise in the timing of interviews in relation to vacation of the housing by the previous occupants. Ideally, candidates should be able to bring their spouses on the interview day and obtain all the information they require to make a decision if they want the job. It is the care and attention to such details of family arrangements on which successful recruitment depends.

Induction

Having checked on references and appointed the new member of staff, it is most important that an adequate induction into the job takes place. A good start is most beneficial but again it requires management time. Although the objectives of the business will have been explained at the interview, they will need to be clearly confirmed when starting employment. Standards of performance, husbandry methods, approach to tidiness and time-keeping all need to be confirmed. Providing a well labelled map of the farm, together with lists of other essential information, assists the settling-in process. As time progresses, performance will have to be checked against the agreed standards, training needs assessed and any difficulties that have arisen discussed in full.

TRAINING

There is no doubt that with few exceptions everyone involved in a farm business, and certainly the management, would benefit from an appropriate form of training. This should improve their performance either at once or in the future, helping the business by increasing output, by reducing costs, or by a combination of the two. Good training helps the individual to identify what he or she is trying to do and enables the job to be done more effectively which leads to additional pride, confidence and satisfaction. Attitudes towards training are important and managers need to demonstrate the above advantages, perhaps coupled with appropriate financial rewards. With some farm activities, e.g. sprayer operation in the UK, tests have to be taken by the operators. Older, skilled staff sometimes have difficulty in seeing any personal benefits from training and many new entrants to the industry fight shy of activities that look like an extension of school. Such employees will probably respond better initially to 'on-farm' training than attendance at specialized centres.

On-farm courses are particularly appropriate to skills training so long as the instructor has the required ability for the job. Many farm workers who are themselves highly skilled operatives, either with machines or in livestock husbandry tasks, are uninterested or perhaps find difficulty in passing on their skills to the average trainee. On the other hand, a particularly bright and motivated trainee can learn much and improve his performance by working with such a person. A further benefit to on-farm training is the availability of resources to enable extended practice of the task in hand. 'Off-farm' training does tend to make better use of instructors' time and, with the easier access to specialized aids, can in many situations be more effective. It is interesting to note, in the UK, the development by the Agricultural Training Board of such sophisticated training aids as a model of a calving cow. A short period working with such an aid can provide wide experience (even if simulated) that would take years for a trainee to obtain in the work situation.

The most successful skills training programme involves regular practice on the farm with an amateur tutor supplemented by a number of short periods at a training centre, supervised by a professional instructor. In the UK, the formation of training groups, in recent years, is proving to be a useful method of on-farm training in that instructors are able to develop specialized knowledge of local situations and use their time in the best possible way.

Training at supervisory level does necessitate periods away from the farm at a specialized centre with tutors implementing a carefully prepared syllabus, tailored to the needs of the group. Matching the needs of an individual to an appropriate course is important, as little is achieved from a course which is either above or below an individual's needs at that time. The fact that staff leave the everyday concerns of the farm for a short period and are in company with similarly situated people, often with identical problems, can in itself be rewarding to them. On return from supervisory level courses, staff should be encouraged to discuss their experiences, explain what they have learned and particularly what they consider can be applied to their job or to other aspects of the farm business. Training prior to future promotion is a wise move in organizations where such possibilities exist, but can lead to frustration if people consider that they are overtrained for the job they are doing.

We do not wish, however, to give the impression that training is the prerogative of operatives. Top level managers have to identify their own weaknesses and also take steps to obtain appropriate corrective action by, for example, obtaining places on advanced farm management courses or on the more specialized courses related to specific management topics. Although the theoretical aspects of management can be covered in such courses and sophisticated aids such as video machines used to simulate practical situations, the opportunities for on-farm practice of management skills are more difficult to obtain. Many top farmers and managers did, in the early part of their career, work under a successful farmer who not only showed them by example, but also took valuable time to explain the reasons behind his actions. Unfortunately, such opportunities are rare, as successful managers tend to be busy managing and sometimes think that they do not have the time to train the next generation.

Training should be an on-going process undertaken as and when appropriate. The introduction of new machinery or a technique to the farm is a time when not only do the operatives need detailed training, but also the manager will need at least an 'awareness' session so that he or she is in the picture and can provide the management back-up which may be necessary at a later date.

MOTIVATION

Farm staff hold the key to productivity, and we need to consider the factors involved in motivating workers to give of their best. Human beings are motivated by their basic needs. First come the 'primitive' needs of food, shelter, safety and security. As the standard of living increases, 'social' needs become more relevant – the need to belong and the need to know that someone cares for their interests. The need of the 'ego' to feel important and to have a sense of achievement are important motivating factors.

Managers need to appreciate that they are dealing with individuals. Each individual will attach his or her own level of importance to such considerations as hours of work, rewards, amenities and even to job satisfaction. Team leaders, be they managers or foremen, need, therefore, to know each member of staff well enough to understand his or her attitudes and relationships with others. The skills and personalities of each individual need to be fitted into the overall plan for the farm so that everyone feels that he or she is a valuable member of an efficient team. Working conditions should allow people to take a pride in their work with their contribution being clearly recognized and fully appreciated and rewarded. The long-standing gulf in the standard of living between farmer and staff, although narrowing, is still a reality in many situations. Despite this, farm workers show tremendous loyalty and are keen to defend 'their' farm against such problems as vandals, poachers or other unwanted callers. Good team spirit is clearly demonstrated by a motivated staff at difficult or crisis times, such as a late harvest. Workers often give up their private commitments to work long hours for the good of the business.

To a proportion of workers, a ladder of opportunity is a motivating force. Such people need to be encouraged to obtain qualifications and take part in training courses. On the other hand, many farm workers are content in their situation and do not want to take additional responsibility.

A subject which cannot be ignored under the heading of motivation is that of incentive payments. We do not wish to go into the pros and cons of incentives in every farming situation but it is our view that they can, in general, cause more problems than they solve. It is notoriously difficult to arrange a scheme which is fair to both parties, which is easily understood, and which clearly reflects the efforts of the individual. So often in present day farming situations, hard work which was traditionally paid on piece-work rates has disappeared in favour of mechanization, and decisions have to be taken by management which affect the performance of an enterprise as much as, if not more than, the efforts of the staff. Indirect payments such as profit-sharing schemes create similar problems and it is, of course, impractical to think about loss-sharing, especially in a difficult year when staff may have put in exceptional effort and yet profits remain low or non-existent. We repeat that we have expressed a personal view here. There is no right or wrong way to proceed. There are situations where incentive payments are made and seem to suit employer and employee alike. This is clearly a matter for each individual farmer and manager to consider and act accordingly.

LEADERSHIP

From our experience in visiting a wide range of farms, it is very clear that there is a close correlation between good farmers and good leaders. Successful leaders have the ability to get the work done through their staff. They are good organizers and create team spirit; their workers know clearly what has to be done and they get on and do it well. Delegation is not only practised but it is a major factor in their success. Although there is so often a close working relationship between the farmer and his staff, this should not prevent employees showing respect for their leader. An efficient business can only operate where there is one leader. Communications are no doubt a key factor in leadership. Not only do managers need to give clear instructions but they also need to be able to listen to communications from staff. If, for example, there are any signs of discontent, this can then be dealt with quickly before it becomes a major issue.

As was mentioned in the chapter on Planning, it is important to involve staff in setting goals, as they are more likely to want to achieve them if they have been party to their preparation. Staff, where possible, should be allowed to control and monitor their own performance but that does not mean that managers do not need to supervise.

Except on small farms where there may be only one employee, staff need to be encouraged to work as a team and not as individuals. Some people find it difficult to ask for help but they should be encouraged to do so as, for example, when moving stock. Many hands not only make light work but also quick and effective work. A feeling of 'them' and 'us' can easily develop between staff working with stock and other outside staff. It is often the case that one group is not aware of the objectives of the other. This sort of problem can be minimized by arranging staff meetings, but unless skilfully chaired such occasions can be good opportunities for the more extrovert members of staff not just to have their say, but also to say it at some length. A better environment for obtaining the opinion of staff is to talk to each one privately, at least once each week, perhaps when handing over the wages, although we appreciate that many farmers now arrange for such payments to be directly credited to employees' bank accounts. Such occasions, however, can be used to enquire of the employee's family or any other items that the employer may be able to help with.

We do not pretend that leadership is a simple matter, and we do not offer any simple recipe. But neither do we think that leaders are only born. Experience, training, the ability to put oneself in the other person's shoes and the ability to learn from one's own mistakes are all important ingredients in acquiring a leadership which, if properly used, will reflect itself throughout the business.

REDUCING STAFF

Sometimes employees leave an organization. They do so when they are retiring, because they are moving to another job or because their employer wants them to leave. In all three situations problems can arise, but this is another function of management to be dealt with appropriately by planning, making decisions and taking action.

Retirement can take place at the normal age when state pension becomes available, earlier, for health reasons, or be delayed, in cases where the person can still cope with the job or if transferred to tasks which are less demanding. Discussions at an early stage not only allow management plans to be made, but also put the mind of the employee at rest. Housing accommodation can be a worry where a family has occupied a tied cottage which is required for replacement staff. Negotiations with local housing authorities well in advance of the expected date of retirement have in many cases helped to obtain rented property. The development of schemes to enable agricultural workers to buy their own houses while still occupying farm cottages would be of considerable benefit to the industry. Staff who have retired usually like to keep in touch with the farm. They enjoy an opportunity to walk the farm or attend a harvest supper or other social occasion.

An employee moving to another job may be doing so as a part of career development and so long as he or she has stayed sufficient time to make a worthwhile contribution to the farm and gives adequate notice, the move should cause few difficulties. On the other hand, he or she may be leaving because the job has proved to be unsatisfactory and management will then have to take oppropriate action as discussed under the section on recruitment.

The situation of a person leaving because the employer wants it that way can cause difficulties and be painful. It is difficult because (fortunately) it does not happen very often and because there are few guidelines on how to deal with the situation. The literature on personnel management is mainly concerned with finding and keeping staff rather than disengaging them. The occasion can be painful because strained relations are often involved and because individuals' private lives are affected.

Employees are asked to leave a farm for one or more of the following reasons:

---

1. *Redundancy.* The choice is between implementing whatever change is necessary for economic reasons as soon as possible, or deferring the change until natural wastage takes place. Alternatively, staff may be transferred within the organization, working hours reduced or surplus labour kept on to make life more tolerable or to permit future expansion. Managers have to find the most appropriate solution to their situation.

2. *Unsatisfactory performance.* Before contemplating disengagement, the employer needs to reassure himself that all has been done to match the skills and abilities of the man to the job to be done.

Appropriate training needs to have been considered as well as the possibility of a more suitable job in another enterprise. Beyond a certain point it may be unfair to keep an unsuitable employee: unfair to him or her, to other staff, to the employer and to the business. Management should then invite the employee to 'look around' and help in a genuine way to find the person a more suitable job. It is essential to observe any laid-down procedures in order to avoid accusations of unfair dismissal.

3. *Personal incompatibility.* Farms, like other organizations, are generally the richer for having a wide variety of talents and dispositions. Employers have to put up with minor disagreements but positive action may be called for if prolonged personality difficulties upset staff motivation.

4. *Instant dismissal.* There are a very limited number of reasons, e.g. proven theft, which might justify instant dismissal. There are other occasions when for some particular reason the employer has had 'enough'. In such situations the presence of witnesses and proof of earlier warnings may be essential to keep within whatever the law requires.

Such problem cases may well be discussed with the representative of the staff union so that the outcome is seen to be fair to all concerned. The reasons for dismissal in such cases need also to be discussed with the rest of the farm staff.

POSITIVE AND NEGATIVE CONTRIBUTIONS TO EFFICIENT STAFFING

We do not want to create the impression, by ending the chapter on the theme of 'reducing staff', that we have a negative attitude to the subject. On the contrary, the problems which are most likely to be encountered in respect of reducing staff numbers will be minimized if the fullest attention is given to the issues which make up the rest of the chapter.

What we have tried to show is that there are many factors which influence the efficiency of labour use on farms, some of which are positive whilst others are negative. These counteracting influences are demonstrated in Fig. 10.2 and what the 'good' employer will be seeking is to concentrate on those ideas and practices which contribute inwards towards 'productive work' – and the positive attitudes that go with it – and to eliminate anything which detracts away from this central aim.

Fig. 10.2. Positive and negative attitudes to efficient staffing.

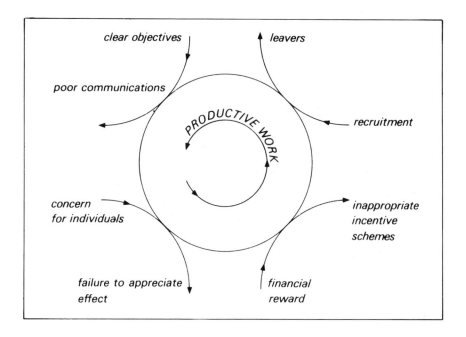

OUR FINAL THOUGHT

There is no more important job for a farmer than taking on a new member of staff. No stone should be left unturned to try to ensure that it is done successfully.

QUESTIONS AND EXERCISES

- Assume that a key member of staff is to leave and that a replacement will be required. Prepared a detailed job description for the post. Compare this with the tasks that the current person actually does.

- Prepare a list of the characteristics of a good leader. Give yourself a score (1 to 10) for each of the items and then consider what you can do to improve on those items with a low score.

- For each member of staff (including family members) give full consideration to their most appropriate training needs for the next two years.

- If you are currently a manager, do you consider that you spend sufficient time inducting new members of staff into the business? Check by having a discussion with the most recent appointee and identify what you could have done to improve the induction process.

GUIDE TO FURTHER READING

Errington, A. (1985) *Delegation on the Farm.* Study No. 8, Reading University Farm Management Unit.
    The most extensive text available on the market.

Farm Management (1971) **2**, No. 1.
    This issue, although somewhat dated, is still relevant and contains a number of very readable articles on staff management in agriculture and in other industries.

Handy, C. B. (1981) *Understanding Organisations*, 2nd edn. Penguin Books, Harmondsworth, London.
    An essential book for those interested in improving their management of people.

Staff Management in Agriculture (1977) MAFF Technical Management Note 22.

MAFF Publications, Pinner, Middlesex.
A most useful guide to the principles of staff management.

Turner, J. and Taylor, M. (1989) *Applied Farm Management.* BSP Professional Books, London.
Chapter 10 describes in some detail the appropriate technique for use in planning labour and machinery requirements.

PART IV

The Manager

Chapter 11

Managing the Manager

The importance of influence
Knowing oneself
The individuality of farm managers
The personal problems of being a farm manager
– Loneliness
– Boredom
– Managerial underemployment
– Use of time
– Delegation
– Working hours
– Recreation
– Insecurity
Finding solutions

THE IMPORTANCE OF INFLUENCE

The style, effectiveness and outward image of any organization is fashioned more by the influence of the person or persons in charge than by anything else. We all recognize this fact, without difficulty, in other organizations: the shops that we buy in; the schools that our children go to; the garages to which we take our car. It is less easy to remember that it also applies to us. The principal aim of this chapter is to remind ourselves of that fact.

The effectiveness with which any farm 'ticks over' is, above all else, a reflection of the competence of its manager, salaried or self-employed. The way in which employees go about their jobs, the extent to which crises occur, the extent, even, to which the weather is allowed to interfere; all of these and many other aspects of a farm business reflect the way the manager manages: his 'management style'. Good planning, good decisions

173

and good control pay dividends in the effectiveness of day-to-day operations; bad planning, bad decisions and bad control do the reverse.

All of that may seem very obvious. The difficult part is remembering
that it applies to **us**! Every manager should remind him or herself from
time to time that he or she is part and parcel of the farm's resources and
not something apart from the land, the capital and the staff. In fact, the
manager is a very important and probably expensive part of those
resources, because of, not despite, his or her special role. The fact that the
manager organizes, directs and controls the total, means that it is his or her
influence that governs the effectiveness with which the combined bundle of
resources is put to work. It is especially important, therefore, to be the most
effective resource of them all; a resource to be controlled along with all the
others. The big difficulty is that the manager has to do it alone.

KNOWING ONESELF

An important part of getting the best out of others – by utilizing their
talents, giving reign to their ambitions and promoting their job satisfaction
– is to try to understand them, develop their strengths and not to aggravate
their weaknesses. If this is true of our dealings with others, it is, no doubt,
equally true of our dealings with ourselves. If we are to draw the best out of
ourselves in the interests of the organization that we manage, some understanding of our own capabilities and limitations, our aspirations and our
fears, will be an essential part of the process. That was implicit in our
earlier consideration of setting objectives and the task of matching available
resources – including the manager – to realistic and obtainable objectives.

We do not offer any short cut in this process of acquiring self knowledge, and to some it will come easier and quicker than to others. Formal
education – both of a general and of a specialized nature – industrial
training, experience in the job and, for many, some form of travel, service
or experience quite outside farming, can each make a contribution to the
full development of the individual. By this we mean having a maturity
which facilitates both self-understanding and a competence to undertake
the management job in hand, including the employment and development
of others. The paths that individuals tread in these matters vary according
to their circumstances and inclinations. There is no single path for an
aspiring manager, but instead varying degrees of education, training and
experience, fusing in different ways for different individuals; with one
phase of life building on another, opening, informing and training the mind
during its most receptive years.

The impact and influence of others on each of us will be of paramount
importance in this process, and it will not be confined to the influence of
those who teach us in a formal sense. It may well be, for instance, that the

greatest single benefit to be derived for farm managers, if and when they attend training courses, will come more from the contacts they enjoy with fellow managers – each with his or her own set of problems – than from any tutor. And it could even be that training courses designed specifically to promote personal growth and development could be as valuable to a young farm manager, or to a farmer's son or daughter needing to assert his or her own individuality, as any form of technical training.

THE INDIVIDUALITY OF FARM MANAGERS

Although each farm manager and farmer is an individual, there are good reasons to believe that they have much in common. In previous publications by one of us (see Further Reading), surveying the personal and professional characteristics of the people who are paid to manage British farms, the question has been posed: 'Is there a typical farm manager?.' In reporting on the results of those surveys, the authors pointed cautiously to certain 'characteristics and attitudes which may perhaps typify many of the farm managers in this country.' They offered an identikit which included the following characteristics:

> ... male; between 30 and 50 years of age; married; with a good secondary education and an agricultural qualification; four or five previous jobs; little or no experience outside the industry; in his first management post by the age of 30; operating on 'large' farms; satisfied with his work, but less satisfied with his terms of employment; and over half of them feeling seriously or slightly under-employed as managers.

From time to time the validity of the identikit has been checked and the fact is that it seems to change little with time. Nevertheless, while pointing to the personal characteristics common to most farm managers the authors also concluded that 'ultimately, of course, *differences* as well as similarities need to be taken into account.'

A wide range of personal and farming circumstances has been represented by the small sample of salaried farm managers in the UK who took part in our surveys, and the range would be still greater if we had included self-employed as well as salaried managers, or those who manage farms elsewhere in the world. However, we have several times expressed the view that the management problems that face farming are very similar to those facing other sectors of the economy. If that is true, how can the strictly 'management' problems encountered on one farm or another – or even in one country or another – differ greatly?

We see these problems as falling into two very broad categories, although the distinction is a fine one. First, there are those problems that are primarily related to managing a farm – the technical, financial and organizational problems discussed in the previous chapters. Secondly, there are those more personal problems that stem from being the manager: problems related to job satisfaction, personal development and responsibility for others. The remainder of this chapter discusses some of these important issues. It is based on a combination of research, observation and discussions that the authors have had with many of those involved.

THE PERSONAL PROBLEMS OF BEING A FARM MANAGER

Loneliness

Farm managers are often intellectually and professionally lonely. This problem results from the fact that farm managers are usually well-educated, well-informed people working in relative isolation. That implies no disrespect whatsoever to their staff, for whom we have the highest regard. Nevertheless the farm manager (self-employed or salaried) is relatively isolated – often very isolated – from his or her peers. Spontaneous consultations and discussion with equals, of the kind that those who work in larger organizations enjoy, are scarce. The individual may or may not feel that this is a disadvantage but some who are known personally to us certainly do, and try to make positive attempts to counteract the situation. This no doubt partly explains why many farmers seem to have an almost insatiable appetite for evening meetings, conferences, farm walks and similar events. The industrial manager or professional man who has been with colleagues all day seems a little less eager for these things. Farmers and farm managers have a genuine need in this respect, but they have to learn how to be discriminating in allocating their time.

Boredom

Strange as it may seem farm managers can get bored. Occasionally, of course, we all can. It might be supposed, however, that the job satisfaction associated with farming makes farmers and farm managers immune from this particular problem. This is not so, and they would not be human if it were. Indeed, the very slowness and in some cases the repetition of certain events, coupled with the isolation we have just discussed, can give rise to it. The likelihood of this happening depends on the individual and the size, nature and complexity of the business concerned; but when it does occur, a careful blend of counterbalancing activities is needed. Getting off the farm, whether for social or professional reasons, can be an important antidote to boredom. So too can attending some form of training course. This should not be a prerogative of employees. It may be of more importance to the long-term survival of a business that from time to time the manager is retrained than that his staff are. Mixing with non-agricultural people can also help. Just filling in time is the worst possible solution.

Managerial underemployment

Closely related to the question of boredom is the fact that farm managers are often in danger of feeling underemployed in the strictly managerial sense. Do not mistake us. We are not saying that they are underemployed in total. The demands on their time and the scope for physical work, if nothing else, ensure that in most cases that is not so. Many farmers and managers have told us, however, that the amount of management input that is required – even on quite large farms, and especially if activities tend to be highly seasonal – does sometimes mean that they are not managerially fully extended. Different individuals cope with this problem in different ways. Some just accept it, and maybe allow Parkinson's Law to take over; others become physically involved in the operation of the farm, and, if there is no obvious alternative, they clearly provide a very convenient form of part-time labour with no 'opportunity cost'; yet others look around for methods of intensifying their farming activities, in some cases to the extent of managing a second farm. The challenge and interest of researching, setting up and managing a new enterprise can be an important antidote to the boredom of routine. Where the opportunity or inclination does not exist the manager might become involved in non-farming activities of various kinds; commercial, political or involving community service. A few, quite sensibly, enjoy recreation. This whole problem is clearly related to that of organizing managerial time – the next topic on our list.

Use of time

Farmers, like many others, often find it difficult to organize their own time. In this, they are often victims of their own circumstances. They manage small businesses; they alone usually represent 'top management', and a wide variety of individuals – either the staff employed on the farm or members of the wide band of ancillary folk with whom farmers have to deal – will want access to 'the gaffer'. The sheer need to be available and to be ready to move from one job to another (often involving considerable travel), ensures that uncommitted time will usually be at a premium. The *ad hoc* nature of supervisory management takes over.

In these circumstances farmers can very easily become too busy doing more pressing things to have time for the important ones. Certainly, there is a lot of time when the manager simply has to be available to others: it is a major part of the job. But it is equally important that there is time available – uninterrupted time – for the important things on which long-term survival may well depend. We do not subscribe to the view that a farm manager has to be available all the time any more than he or she has to be able to do every job on the farm. A manager has his or her own job to do, and more than anything else it is to ensure that there continues to be a job for others. Drucker talks in *The Effective Executive* about 'discretionary time'; we talk about 'usable chunks of time': days or half days regularly set aside when the manager is not available to others; it is as if he or she was away. The manager has a pressing appointment – with him or herself, and the farm office may not be the most sensible place in which to try to keep it! If a manager wishes to bring about this state of affairs he or she must do it alone. No one else will help him. If the reader feels that this is required in their own case then they will need to look critically at how they use their time and restructure it a little so that the necessary number of 'usable chunks of time' are made available. A degree of firmness will be required which will only be present if the individual concerned wants it to be. Farm staff will understand, if the matter is explained to them properly. Tell them that you are ensuring that their jobs will continue to be there, and recruit their assistance by delegating authority to them. They will respond to both of these things.

Delegation

Farmers, on the whole, are not good delegators. That should not be surprising. In small businesses the scope for delegation – maybe even the need for it – is often slight. Many farmers, therefore, get little practice, and practice, as in all things, makes perfect. Delegation is an art. It is not simply a matter of telling someone else to get on with a job that you do not want to do. Several steps are involved:

1. Identifying the job and the responsibility involved;
2. Identifying the right individual to do it;
3. Instructing him or her and giving the appropriate authority to get on with it; and
4. Getting out of the way so that he or she can get on with it, in his or her own manner – leaving him or her alone but maintaining a correct degree of interest and support as and when required.

This whole process of delegation is not easy and should not be undertaken lightly. But it is important to look for opportunities to delegate in a responsible way. It will help in the development of the careers and capability of others. It will also help to provide the freedom for the manager to undertake the various important tasks of management upon which – as we have repeatedly said – the survival of a business may ultimately depend. Delegation can also help to remedy the vexed question, in farming, of long and often anti-social hours.

Working hours

Farmers perhaps accept long, irregular hours and short holidays too readily. We have spoken to their spouses, as well, and know this to be true! It can have serious repercussions on family life. Sometimes, of course, it is inevitable and essential. Too often, however, it is associated with 'living over the shop', with a mistaken feeling of indispensability and a reluctance or inability to delegate properly. We know more than one farmer who lives in a town house and who literally goes to work from nine to five. We are not suggesting this would suit all, but we are suggesting that long hours of work can become a problem to which a sensible and balanced solution should be found. All work and no play. . . .

Recreation

Farmers, as a breed, are not renowned for having regular recreational outlets. These are necessary in order to get away from the business and from farming, into a totally different and relaxing activity with fresh company. We cannot overestimate the importance of this; it should preferably be an activity which involves a firm commitment, rather than one that you can choose to do if it is a pleasant day and you are not too busy when the time arrives. The rejuvenating effect of this kind of commitment – no matter what it is – will pay dividends when you return. You will see things in a better perspective: minor problems will be seen for what they are. Other people, to whom you have delegated responsibility, will have managed in your absence. They will have enjoyed the responsibility vested in them and responded to it.

Insecurity

Finally, there are various ways in which farmers and farm managers, like everyone else, can feel professionally insecure. This can arise from various reasons, quite apart from the normal anxieties of generating the expected or required profit. Uncertainties – and therefore insecurity – may stem from a failure to have a clear idea of the immediate path ahead, either because the individual concerned has found it difficult to identify his objectives and his subsequent plans, or because, in the case of the salaried manager, his employer has not encouraged this approach. Insecurity can also arise from a lack of professional confidence. This is closely associated with the whole question of personal growth and will clearly affect some individuals more than others. It will usually lessen with advancing age. We believe, however, that more than a few farmers have a problem of this kind.

Managerially speaking, their circumstances are inclined to create a situation in which they can become jack-of-all-trades and masters of none. They may not, for instance, talk with the authority of the banker, the personnel manager, the sales manager or the production manager whom they meet in industry. This can and does sometimes create feelings of inferiority. It should not do so. The farmer's circumstances are entirely different from those of the specialists just referred to and it is our view that when compared with their true counterparts in the rest of the economy – general managers of other small businesses – farming's managers have no need to feel in any way inferior.

There is also that other kind of insecurity that is sometimes the lot of the salaried manager. His or her employment is dependent upon the financial and family circumstances, and even the personal whims, of the employers. We do not know many 'old' farm managers, and have known some sad instances of dismissal. Salaried managers are too small a group to exert much political influence on their own behalf, try as they might. We believe, however, that in the UK at least, the combination of legal safeguards against wrongful dismissal, the creation of provision against redundancy, and a growing awareness on the part of the employers of farm managers of the need for proper career opportunities through contracts of employment, promotion prospects and pension schemes will all gradually improve the situation. But there is still a long way to go in this, even in this country – and some managers may (and do) feel the need to plan alternative and second careers before insuperable difficulties arise.

FINDING SOLUTIONS

This account of some of the personal problems that are likely to beset the manager of a farm may seem depressingly long and dismal. It is not intended to be. Farmers and farm managers do not constitute an inadequate group of individuals incapable of dealing with the normal buffetings that their occupation and life deal out. It is simply that the problems that have been discussed here frequently do exist, and can easily militate against the full and effective development of the individual concerned. That in turn makes him or her a less effective manager than he or she might otherwise have been, and that in turn influences the effectiveness of the other people and resources employed in that business. Ultimately profits suffer – with serious consequences. We do not wish to dramatize the situation but feel it is important that the possibility (indeed the probability) of some of these problems existing should be recognized.

We have hinted at possible answers to these problems. There may, of course, be no precise answers. Whatever answers individuals find, however, will reflect something of their own personalities and the environments in which they find themselves. Geographical differences between regions as well as between countries will have important influences. In almost all cases, however, answers to the kinds of problems and issues that have been discussed here will be *human* in character rather than *technical* or *financial.* Perhaps the most important factor is that the existence of these problems should be recognized and openly discussed. That will go a long way towards providing an answer. The manager will then be on the way to managing him or herself.

OUR FINAL THOUGHT

There is no short cut to competence. Education, training, experience on the job and contact with others all play their part – and with them come maturity and judgement.

QUESTIONS AND EXERCISES

- Make a list of these aspects of managing your farm that you find most personally demanding. In each case ask yourself why, and consider what you can do to ease the situation.

- Make a list of what you find most difficult about managing yourself. Then, in each case, consider what you can do about it.

- Consider each of the eight problems discussed in this chapter. Identify how far they are relevant to you and consider in each case what action you should take.

- Identify one task that you are currently responsible for that you would like to delegate – then, following the procedure set out in this chapter, implement the delegation.

- Keep some spot checks on how you use your time. Critically examine the evidence and consider how you might beneficially reorganize your work and leisure routines.

GUIDE TO FURTHER READING

Atkinson, M. J. (1987) *Your Management Style in Management Matters in 1987.*
Farm Management Unit Study Report No. 14, University of Reading.
Sets out the range of management style.

Ansell, D. J. (1970) The farmer and his time. *Farm Management* **1**, No. 8, 36–43.
An account of a mini Rosemary Stewart-type survey, conducted amongst
farmers in Berkshire. Would assist anyone thinking of keeping their own
timesheets.

Armstrong, M. (1983) *How to be a Better Manager.* Kogan Page, London.
A complete A-Z of managerial skills but relevant to the whole field of 'personal performance'.

Garratt, S. (1985) *Manage Your Time.* Fontana/Collins, London.
Gets down to brass tacks.

Giles, A. K. and Mills, F. D. (1970) *Farm Managers.* Miscellaneous Study No. 47
Dept of Agricultural Economics and Management, University of Reading.
The first of a series of such studies.

Pedler, M. and Boydel, T. (1985) *Managing Yourself.* Fontana/Collins, London.
Well worth reading, especially the last chapter.

Stewart, P. (1970) *Managers and their jobs.* Pan Books, London.
A readable account of how 160 managers spend their time in industry.

Chapter 12

Acquiring Information

A universal need
Kinds of information
    – technical
    – financial
    – legal
    – international trade
    – the environment
Sources of information
Market intelligence data
Storage and retrieval
Advisers and consultants
Investment of time

A UNIVERSAL NEED

One aspect of management which is especially important for the manager to manage himself is the provision of information. Here, in particular, the manager needs to be well organized. We have, therefore, decided to devote a separate chapter to this subject and to place it in this final part of our book.

In the course of discussing various aspects of the management task, reference has been made to the importance of having the appropriate information. Indeed, the four major management functions outlined in Part II, and the four areas of a business outlined in Part III, are all, in some way or another, dependent upon the information that is available to a manager. The need is universally felt across the business.

Thus, *setting objectives* for the business involves having a knowledge of the many factors which determine the environment in which the business has to operate. Managers need to involve themselves in a certain amount of reading, listening and conversing with others so as to be aware of the economic, political and increasingly the environmental, constraints under which they have to manage their business.

The *planning process* involves using relevant physical and financial data obtained from both within and outside the farm. Non-quantitative information is in many circumstances just as important as quantitative. It may, for example, indicate that, once fully evaluated, one method of production eases the stress on management and workers compared with another.

Decision-making clearly depends upon the availability of relevant information. It is an integral part of the task whether the decisions be of a strategic or tactical nature.

Control is similarly only possible when information is to hand. Control has to be 'against' something. Again, this may be quantitative data in respect of inputs or outputs or it may include a wide range of other information, such as the cloddiness of a seedbed or the morale of staff, which will have a direct bearing on the control of day-to-day operations.

Management of the four areas of the business – production, finance, marketing or staffing – also clearly necessitates having information that is appropriate to any particular matter in hand. We will now consider the kinds of information to be acquired, their sources, and the methods by which this information can be obtained and stored, in a little more detail.

KINDS OF INFORMATION

We have identified five main categories of information that a farmer requires: technical, financial, legal, international and environmental.

Technical

From the point of view of production, if farm enterprises are to be profitable they need, in the first instance, to be technically efficient. Prices of inputs and outputs are obviously very important, but we cannot stress too firmly that farmers are in the business of production in a technical way. New developments are continually being made available, and the farmer must be able to obtain detailed information in order to evaluate the likely benefit of such developments in his or her particular situation.

Take, for instance, the dairy farmer selecting a bull from the AI organizations from which to breed herd replacements. Published information is available relating to proven sires which indicate the improvements to be expected in the daughters of a bull over their contemporaries in terms of milk yield, quality and conformation as well as such features as a tendency to produce heavy calves and associated calving difficulties. The bull may have a sufficiently high 'weighting' indicating that an adequate number of daughters has been tested in a wide spread of herds to give the data adequate statistical significance. Nevertheless, the farmer will also take opportunities to inspect as wide a selection of the daughters as possible and at the same time to see the dams so as to be sure just how well the bull is correcting conformation faults. The prospective user may also want to discuss with the owner of the cattle subjects such as temperament and slowness of milking. This kind of information is somewhat difficult to report in print. Visits to agricultural shows or to breeders' farms take time, but they are of value, especially to herdsmen who will eventually have to milk and manage the offspring being planned. Some breeding companies produce video films of progeny which avoids the need for travelling. This example underlines the fact that although considerable published information may be available to a manager on any particular subject, it is a good idea, to obtain the views of other experienced people.

Many cereal farmers, for example, have in recent years joined a local or regional group, and in return for their subscriptions receive detailed and up-to-date information on varieties and optimum input levels from trials carried out under similar soil and climatic conditions to their farms. This information is confidential to members and if advisers or agronomists wish to join and so use the information more widely, then increased levels of subscription are usually charged.

Financial

The preparation of the accounts and balance sheet summarizing what has happened require information, much of which should be readily available from the farm books. Budgeting and capital appraisal, both looking to the future, demand information from a wide range of sources both on and off the farm. As with technical information, relevance to the particular situation is of major importance. Financial data has a more private nature than most other kinds, and there is no substitute, in our minds, for good 'on the farm' data as a basis for future thinking.

The subject of borrowing will serve here as an example. Although the banks may regularly advertise their services, it is not until the farmer makes a personal approach to the bank that he or she will find out if he or she is able to borrow, how much and on what terms. The response to a request will depend on the national economic climate and the farmer's net worth. It will also depend upon the feasibility of the particular project, the detailed way in which the proposal has been prepared and how relevant the figures are to the actual situation being discussed. The response may also vary from one bank to another; not that farmers should regularly change their bankers. In general, if a farmer needs financial assistance from any lender, a considerable amount of homework will have to be done before a positive response is obtained.

Legal

Managers of farms, as well as managers of other sectors of the economy, have to operate within the legal framework of the country in which they do business. The task of getting oneself acquainted with all the necessary legislation is not an easy one and it is made more difficult by constant additions and changes to the statute book. The law affects many aspects of operating a farm of which taxation, employment, safety, road traffic and environmental planning are but a few.

Ignorance is no excuse in the eyes of the law. Managers must therefore be able to recognize when proper legal advice is required. Solicitors' fees will be unnecessarily high if they are called on too soon but court and lawyers' costs could be even greater if they are called on too late. Membership of such organizations as the National Farmers Union or Producer Associations does prove valuable in obtaining expert advice, and a file headed 'Useful Legal Information' is also worth keeping.

For those investigating the feasibility of introducing an enterprise, such as the conversion of redundant farm buildings for holiday letting, the employment of an appropriate consultant could be the most efficient method of obtaining the necessary legal information.

A more common example is the need for farmers to be aware of the legislation in the UK relating to trailer brakes. The law states that all trailers over a minimum weight need to be fitted with a braking system which can be operated from the tractor driver's seat. In practice, considerable difficulties arise with modern safety cabs and because of the need for quick release couplings when trailers are being constantly changed, for instance, when making silage. Despite these problems, managers know that the safety of their drivers is of paramount importance and that efficient trailer braking is imperative. To keep within the law in all situations may seem virtually impossible, but to be ignorant of it is, as we have said, no excuse.

International trade

A considerable range of inputs into the UK farm business is imported and an expanding number of commodities are sold into the world market. Some farmers will therefore need to have some awareness of the international market conditions, of exchange rates, levies and subsidies. Normally, they will not be dealing directly with an overseas customer but through a dealer, as in the case of machinery imports, or an agent, as with exports. This middleman will monitor the trading situation and provide the information as part of the service.

Those planning to trade within the EC can obtain appropriate information from specialized journals such as *Agri.Europe*. When full harmonization of the regulations has been achieved as a result of the Single Market implementation, the current risks involved in changing 'green currency' will be minimized. Farmers may wish to back their own judgement and follow, for example, the international situation for a particular commodity (e.g. soya bean) before placing an order with their merchant. Similarly, lowland sheep farmers could observe the higher prices of, say, finished lamb that are being obtained in another country, especially for carcasses of a certain weight, conformation and lean meat content. They might then consider ways of cashing in on such a trade and begin by evaluating new breeds of 'terminal' rams to produce the required carcasses. They may even need to look at such factors as a change of lambing date, feeding system or even breed of ewe in order to meet the needs of the export buyer.

The environment

As with the legal situation, the need to be aware of environmental requirements is an area of increasing significance to the farmer. An increasing number of aspects of this subject are covered by the law, whereas others involve a moral obligation to the community. All farmers can do their part in helping to conserve the countryside. These contributions help to:

1. Maintain a pleasant environment for their families and staff as well as for the community;
2. Conserve the diversity of wildlife for the benefit of future generations;
3. Enhance the landscape, for example with features that replace the vast number of elm trees destroyed by Dutch elm disease;
4. Retain our heritage as a living record of the evolution of the countryside.

These objectives can best be achieved by the farmer and staff taking care at all times to avoid husbandry operations which have an adverse impact on the environment of the farm. Using the local Farming and Wildlife Advisory Group (FWAG) adviser to help identify the more important landscape, wildlife and historic features of the farm can be most advantageous. It may even be possible to add new features such as a pond or group of trees, at minimal cost, by using 'spare' labour in less busy periods of the year.

In the UK, codes of practice are published in respect of such aspects of animal welfare and aerial spraying of pesticides. Another example of an activity covered by this heading is the burning of straw by arable farmers. A code of practice is available, local bye-laws are involved and considerable advisory information has been published on the subject of stubble burning. To follow the code precisely, for instance ensuring timely incorporation of the ash, causes considerable effort and inconvenience to both farmer and staff, as well as cost to the business. If short cuts are taken, disasters are more likely to occur and pressure will increase for the practice to be banned. There is always the concern, in situations where the profit objective is given too much priority, that corners are likely to be cut. But there are objectives to running a farm business other than profits and an important one is that of caring for the environment.

SOURCES OF INFORMATION

A word or two now about the sources from which farmers obtain information. There is a wide variety so it is important that each farmer explores the range and finds the most convenient sources. Much will depend on how much time he or she is prepared to allocate to reading, making visits and attending conferences. Managers of small scale businesses may well be involved in manual chores for a large proportion of the working day, and at other times be too tired to concentrate on serious reading.

Radio broadcasts on the other hand can be listened to while working, even in farm buildings or using portable sets in tractor cabs. Taped information is already available and could be more widely used especially by 'working' managers. Television is a good medium for gaining ideas but is seldom suited to obtaining detailed data. The use of videotapes is increasing significantly, especially for training purposes.

The written word continues to be a major source of information and the farming industry, especially in the UK, is well served with publications of many kinds. Many daily papers, especially provincial issues, carry farming information with reports, news and feature articles, and popular weekly publications fulfil this role in a comprehensive way. Specialized publications, usually on a monthly basis, deal well with many aspects of the major enterprises as well as machinery and management topics. A considerable proportion of this material is paid for by advertising revenue and is available free to farmers. This is perhaps a mixed blessing as free material more easily finds its way into the waste paper basket.

Numerous institutions, including government departments, universities and research institutes, produce a comprehensive range of publications, as do the trade and the banks. One problem is knowing what is available. The situation can be helped by membership of an organization, such as the

Centre for Management in Agriculture or the British Institute of Management, which produce lists of available information and literature reviews.

MARKET INTELLIGENCE DATA

This subject embraces several different kinds of information. The agricultural industry in many countries, but especially in the UK, is well served with a market reporting service. Material is available from the farming and local press, in radio broadcasts, as well as from telephone dial-in recorded messages. Usually, this information reports recent sale prices with some indication as to type or grade of commodity. Many producers are in direct contact with the market on a regular basis in respect of both buying and selling, however, so do not need to study such published material.

In general, there is a lack of information available to farmers about expected market situations in the future. Such information is required when planning production and when making investment decisions. If such information were available, no doubt this would cause over-reaction with many commodities and the outcome would be very different to that first predicted. Hunt (1974), in the article in *Farm Management* referred to at the end of this chapter, suggests two promising lines of approach to overcome this problem. First, to set up reporting arrangements to keep track of response and to report continuously. The MAFF quarterly report goes some way towards this in respect of critical items such as in-pig gilts. Secondly, he suggests that products which are subject to 'over response' could be increasingly marketed through groups of cooperatives which have a ready contact with the changing state of the market.

The task of obtaining all the necessary marketing information and interpreting it correctly is not an easy one. It is also time consuming so that many farmers may be well advised to concentrate on production and to delegate the major part of marketing to the specialists. These may be the enthusiastic leaders of producer groups for buying and selling, full-time employees of cooperatives or specialized marketing consultants. Seldom will the official adviser consider that this type of activity comes into his or her court.

STORAGE AND RETRIEVAL

It is becoming increasingly common for a farmer to obtain information for a particular purpose by the use of a telephone link to a central or local computerized data base. Such information as, for example, the nearest location of a required machinery part, can be obtained as a printout or by display on a VDU. Broadcasting authorities also offer a wide range of televised data sheets. It may be that the farmer requires data relating to his or her own business or to the national or even international situation. For many, especially smaller farm businesses, it will continue to be more appropriate to accumulate all such required information in the farm office. A good, usable, system of filing data is then essential. It may be based on individual cost items or enterprises: it is very much a matter for the individual. But it is important to be able to access the data and information when necessary. Such data needs to be kept up to date and to be readily available for reference. Some managers consider the analysis of farm data to be a job that they need to do personally as it helps them to quickly pinpoint areas needing control action. Others delegate this task to office staff and make decisions based on summaries. There is a real need for the person collating and analysing farm data to have the necessary skills and experience as accuracy is vital. This may well involve close contact with staff who collect the raw data, so as to be in a position to quickly clear any queries that may arise.

Information received from outside the business must be stored, but must also be available for speedy reference. Filing of journals and market reports by date of issue causes few problems, but more difficult is the retrieval of an interesting article on a particular topic read in a magazine months ago. It is useful to keep a set of box files labelled by enterprise or subject. Interesting articles which may be of use in the future are cut or torn out at the time of reading and stored in this way. Piles of back numbers of journals and magazines that you intend to read, have a habit of growing uncontrollably high.

ADVISERS AND CONSULTANTS

We have already discussed the valuable role that an outsider can have in assisting a manager to set clear objectives and in planning the strategy for the business. Here consider the wider role of the adviser or consultant. Amongst the most important contributions they can offer are:

---

1. Specialist technical information, such as the identification of crop disease and recommendations for control. Such a specialist may well be retained by a group of producers to visit their farmers on a regular basis and offer assistance at production level in respect of selection of inputs and timeliness of operations.
2. Guidance on technical aspects, especially in relation to setting up a new enterprise, including full feasibility studies. The inseparability of technical and managerial aspects of farming may require the expertise of a widely experienced consultant.

3. Advice of a strictly economic nature, perhaps involving analysis of past performance, or future planning or questions of capital procurement and appraisal.

4. The use of his 'trained eye' to give opinion, either to confirm the views of the farmer or to help overcome the fact that the farmer may be too close to his business to view it objectively.

5. Specialized guidance in one of the more complicated aspects of business management, such as taxation or recruitment of staff.

6. Specialist advice on the establishment of new, perhaps alternative, enterprises involving particular aspects of marketing.

7. Regular consultations over a period of time to assist in the implementation of control procedures.

Regular contact with an adviser can build a relationship of mutual trust and understanding so that follow-up advice becomes even more valuable. As time progresses, the advice will often become more involved with the whole farm business so that the outside influence is then considerable.

INVESTMENT OF TIME

The amount of information that any farmer might need and the range of sources from which it is available present a rather frightening prospect. What we have tried to suggest is that each individual needs to think through this topic and devise a strategy to meet his or her own needs and circumstances. In any particular situation there are certain obvious needs and certain obvious sources. It is a good idea to identify and concentrate on these, and to set priorities. Sometimes the required information will come from deliberate attempts to collect it, at other times it will be a by-product of some other activity, such as a discussion, a farm walk or the like, hence the value of keeping a notebook and pen to hand at all times. It is important for each individual to learn how much time can be spared for this kind of activity. Under- or over-involvement to the detriment of the many other chores could be dangerous, and finding the right balance is not at all easy.

OUR FINAL THOUGHT

Farm managers need specific information, not large arrays of data, that will help them to manage. They need to learn where to get it, how to store and retrieve it, and how to use it.

QUESTIONS AND EXERCISES

- Devote some time (a half-day) to examining your office and information storage systems – and decide how it could be improved so as to save you time and give you better information.

- Carry out a check over the next month on how much of the material that comes through your letterbox you (a) read, (b) do not read, and (c) should read. What should you now do about it?

- Do you have a ready-to-hand, up-to-date list of names and telephone numbers for you, or for others in your absence, to refer to in case of emergencies? If not, prepare it sooner rather than later!

- Think carefully about the advisers you use, or could use, to help improve the effectiveness of each of your enterprises and the profit from the whole business. Satisfy yourself that this list meets your needs and is likely to continue to bring benefits to your business in the foreseeable future.

GUIDE TO FURTHER READING

Bakewell, K. G. B. (1984) *How to Organise Information.* Gower, Aldershot.
   Provides very useful advice for managers on how to deal with all the information that comes their way.

Brown, D. (1973) Farm office organisation. *Farm Management* **2**, No. 5.
   A useful guide to office procedures.

Giles, A. K. (1970) Management consultants. *Agriculture* **77**, No. 11, 525–8.
   This short article discusses the need for and the value of farm advice.

Hunt, K. E. (1974) Market intelligence – which way now? *Farm Management* **2**, No. 8, 435–41.
   A valuable article for readers interested in the use of information relating to the market function.

Moverley, J. (1986) *Microcomputers in Agriculture.* Collins, London.
   Chapter 9 explains how computers can be of help in the farm business to obtain and use vital information.

Turner, K. and Bury, P. (1989) Who's who in the Countryside. *Farm Management* **7**, No. 3.
   A helpful guide to the main organizations involved with the UK countryside.

Chapter 13

Priorities

The importance of priorities
The nature of priorities
Ordering the priorities
Sticking with priorities

THE IMPORTANCE OF PRIORITIES

This chapter is short but important: it is about getting the most important things done.

In his stimulating book, *The Effective Executive*, Peter Drucker suggests that it is possible for executives actually to develop habits of mind which will help to make them more effective; that over and above the normal attributes of intelligence, imagination and knowledge, effectiveness can be learned. He lists five habits of mind to be cultivated in order to help bring this situation about. One of these is to identify priorities and to stay with them. In order to try to capture something of the flavour of what Drucker has to say on this topic we have strung together some of his phrases from the relevant chapters:

> effective executives concentrate on the few major areas where superior performance will produce outstanding results ... They know that they have no choice but to do first things first and second things not at all. The alternative is to get nothing done ... If there is any one 'secret' of effectiveness, it is concentration. Effective executives do first things first and they do one thing at a time ... most of us find it hard enough to do well even one thing at a time, let alone two ... those people who do so many things, and apparently so many difficult things do only one at a time. As a result they need much less time in the end than the rest of us ... effective executives do not race. They set an easy pace but keep going steadily.
>
> (Drucker, 1970, pp. 24–5, pp. 102–5)

We are in total sympathy with these views and know the importance in our own work of being selective. This theme has already run through a number of chapters in this book. It was implicit, for instance, in all that was written about setting objectives – the need to identify what one is aiming at both personally and professionally. The jigsaw of objectives contained in that chapter is essentially about priorities. They appear again in the context of decision-making when, sooner or later, a choice between alternatives has to be made; also in the chapter on Planning in order to avoid management by crisis; and yet again in the chapter on Control in the identification of key results areas – keeping tabs on what really matters.

THE NATURE OF PRIORITIES

We have several kinds of priorities in mind. First, there are those broad priorities related to long term strategies. 'What is needed', says Drucker elsewhere in his book, 'is the right strategy rather than razzle-dazzle tactics.' This interpretation of priorities is virtually synonymous with the concept of management by objectives. Organizing a business or ordering your own personal life means identifying priorities. 'Get your priorities right', we say to each other when discussing broad questions of what matters to us and what does not. It is important, as we noted in our chapters on Objectives and on Managing the Manager, to make enough time available to consider the important things. No manager who wishes to be effective must become too busy dealing with the urgent to deal with the important. Getting the farm plan right for the immediate years ahead is always very important – and especially so in difficult, tight economic times.

There is a second kind of priority; which is identifying the critical areas of a business – what really makes it tick – and keeping careful control over them. As we have already stated earlier in the book, it is very often the case that only a very few key result areas (one, two or three) are the critical ones in determining whether ultimate profits are good, bad or indifferent in a particular year. These priority areas should be identified and given all the managerial time and effort that they demand: food conversion in intensive livestock enterprises; cultivations and the management of plant growth on a cereals farm; milk yield and stocking density in the dairy. Budgetary control, discussed in Chapter 6, is very much about this aspect of management; about doing the important things well.

A third kind of priority relates closely to decision-making. At particular points of time, in the middle of a production cycle, problems arise and a choice between alternatives has to be made. Do you press on with a suspect machine or stop to get it repaired? By what method will you harvest those potatoes in unusually wet conditions? Do you stop an important job to do another (e.g. repairing a broken fence) which may, or may not, create further problems? These are examples of the more pressing and immediate situations in which 'what matters most' has to be identified and dealt with.

There is, finally, a fourth kind of priority situation, when, for instance, a real crisis occurs, perhaps involving personal accident or fire. In these cases priorities become starkly clear. There is no real problem of choice; everything else stops.

ORDERING THE PRIORITIES

When it comes to the ordering of priorities of any kind it is impossible to offer detailed guidance; answers will vary according to individuals and circumstances. Sometimes, as in our fourth situation, answers really will be starkly clear; sometimes, as in the first, they will emerge only after prolonged thought and discussions. In between, situations requiring constant control and firm decisions will require concentration and application. It may help, however, to keep in mind two points. First, the simple question, 'What really matters?'. Robert Townsend tells us in *Up the Organisation* that he keeps a sign opposite his desk which reads, 'Is what I'm doing or about to do getting us closer to our objectives?'. Try applying that question when you next have to decide on a priority. What may also help is to remember that what is deferred very often diminishes in importance and sometimes does not get done at all. If you do not believe us, what about all those articles and reports that you have put on one side to read later? The problem confronting most managers is not simply a matter of selecting the most important task; there are usually too many of those to choose from. It is more often a question of deciding which ones will matter least if they do not get done.

STICKING WITH PRIORITIES

Remembering Drucker's advice about doing one thing at a time, we wish to stress the importance of concentrating on priorities once they have been identified. If this is not done, the whole process will have been a waste of time. On most farms, with their several enterprises, with the problems of distance and the risk of interruptions of the kind discussed in our chapter on Managing the Manager, there is plenty of scope for getting diverted. A lot of time can be spent – and wasted – turning and moving from one job to another. Concentrating on one until it is finished – especially when it has priority – and then moving to the next job on the list has much to commend it. There are those who work well when they have several jobs in hand at the same time, but the possibility of none of them being satisfactorily completed must always be there. In our own experience we are aware of the beneficial effect on morale of actually finishing a job, especially if it has been done well. There is a better chance of that being the case if other things have not been allowed to interfere. Lists of jobs are a valuable aid to getting things in the right order of priority and then getting them done. We could not last without our notebooks! Crossing jobs off the list is very satisfying, and prevents it from just getting longer and longer. The reader should not be apologetic about keeping a list, nor let other people decide for him what should go on it; he should keep his priorities under review – they can change from day to day – and not let others prevent him from completing jobs. If the list just gets longer and longer it's time to do some more delegating!

OUR FINAL THOUGHT

Drucker is right! 'Correct strategies not razzle-dazzle tactics'.

QUESTIONS AND EXERCISES

- Write down the most important long-term strategic priorities for your business.

- What aspects of the enterprises that you have are the key results areas, and which therefore deserve priority?

- If you have not already done so (see Chapter 3) draw a jigsaw of your professional and personal objectives and then decide on your priorities in reaching a satisfactory balance between the two.

- Answer the following questions:
  - How do you go about deciding on your day-to-day priorities?
  - Do you stick at a job until it is completed? Or are you too easily diverted?
  - Do you keep systematic lists of what you have to do?
  - Do crises often occur in your business?
  - Do you always seem to be in a hurry?
  From your answers, what do you conclude about your management?

- Get a pocket notebook and use it!

GUIDE TO FURTHER READING

Drucker, P. F. (1970) *The Effective Executive.* Heinemann, London; Pan Books, London.
  Read Chapter 5 (First things first), but the whole book is priceless. Get it – and read it – regularly.

Townsend, R. (1970) *Up the Organisation.* Michael Joseph Ltd, London; also (1971) Coronet Books, London.

There is, in our view, no real need for other references on this topic but Peters and Waterman's *In Search of Excellence* (see references to Chapter 2) provides an excellent general insight into what makes some businesses successful.

Chapter 14

Summary, Afterthoughts and Conclusions

What has been included and excluded
Inter-relationships in management
Complexities of the task
Our final thoughts
Spouses
Computers
The environment
Managers, not super-managers
Profits
Judgement
Getting it all right

In this final chapter we aim to do three things:

1. To provide a brief summary and to offer our 'final thoughts' on each topic we have discussed
2. To add a few comments on three particular aspects of farm management which have largely escaped our net: spouses, computers and the environment
3. To offer a few concluding thoughts – our 'final final thoughts'!

SUMMARY

What has been included and excluded

We made it clear in our introductory chapter that this book was being written primarily for those who manage farms, in whatever capacity – although we hoped it would be of value also to many others who work with them; and to students. We made it clear also that we were not writing a book about husbandry, about agricultural economics in its broadest sense, not about management techniques in the narrow sense, but about those aspects of management thinking and procedures which occupy the time and attention of anyone who manages a farm.

This means that we have been conscious throughout the writing of this book of its omissions and the fact that we deliberately turned our backs on the inclusion of its many techniques and figures. The book may be unique for that, if for no other reasons. There may be readers who regret that they have not found more illustrations, more husbandry recommendations and more economic theory. If so, we can only plead that our sights were set firmly on the managerial problems that confront farmers and managers. We wanted to provide guidelines not answers, directions not decisions. Whatever other shortcomings our efforts may have, we feel that we can at least claim to have kept to our intentions.

Inter-relationships in management

We have also been conscious throughout of the inter-relationships and the inter-locking nature of our subject and the possibility, therefore, of some duplication of thought. We have been unable to avoid this, and indeed, had we done so, might have wrongly portrayed a subject whose component parts are inter-dependent and inter-locking. Every part of it does seem to us to be equally important. Yet we have been aware that each chapter has seemed to be the most important of them all! Several times we have claimed for different topics – control, production, and finance, for instance, that they are 'at the heart of farming'. The truth of the matter is that each of them is, but each is related to each other.

Complexities of the task

We have made numerous references to the complexity of managing small businesses – with limited scope for delegation – and farms clearly come into this category. We have long possessed a very healthy respect for those who manage commercial farms. Their job is complex; it requires a wide range of expertise and they are relatively isolated in the managerial role. And as we have written this book, spelling out the full complexity of that job, our respect has increased. But those of them whom we know seem to enjoy their lives, despite the problems. We respect them for the job that they do, in all its complexity.

Our final thoughts

In writing about that complexity we needed first to adopt a framework that would describe what is involved. That framework needed to be comprehensive and yet remain uncluttered. The result was the diagram around which our second chapter 'About Management' was based – and in order to encapsulate our main thoughts we have reproduced below 'our final thoughts' on each topic, starting with the second chapter:

About management

It may be more helpful to think in terms of management applied to farms than of farm management as a subject in its own right; farmers and farm managers should avoid thinking of themselves as managerially unique.

Setting objectives

Success will not follow just because objectives have been set. It will follow if those objectives are good ones and if, as far as possible, they are then achieved.

Planning

Planning promotes flexibility not rigidity.

Decision-making

A good manager learns to recognize when an issue or problem deserves time, and then to give it; a too hastily made 'right' decision to a 'wrong' question is a bad use of time. Judgement will be a key ingredient in the decision-making process.

Control

Effective control requires measurement, and when necessary and possible, corrective action; without this action there is no control. There is probably more scope for increasing profits on most farms by a more careful control of the existing system than from radically changing it.

Production

Management is about deciding what you want to do and then doing it. A vital aspect of any production programme lies in determining how much of each enterprise you can 'do'. Changes in economic circumstances have always created changes in attitudes about this – and always will.

Buying and selling

If nobody sells, nothing happens!

Finance

It may help the prospective borrower to prepare his case if he thinks himself into the position of the prospective lender. All of the questions that will be asked will become obvious.

Staff

There is no more important job that a farmer does than when he takes on a new member of staff. No stone should be left unturned to try to ensure that it is done successfully.

Managing the manager

There is no short cut to competence. Education, training, experience on the job and contact with others all play their part, and with them comes maturity of judgement.

Acquiring information

Farm managers need specific information, not large arrays of data, that will help them to manage. They need to learn where to get it, how to store and retrieve it, and how to use it.

Priorities

Drucker is right! 'Correct strategies, not razzle-dazzle tactics'.

AFTERTHOUGHTS

The fact that the three topics mentioned here are described as 'after-thoughts' in no way diminishes them in importance. On the contrary – they are singled out here for special mention before we end.

Spouses

We have already made clear our respect for farm managers. We also respect their spouses (usually wives, but women may be farm managers too!). Those of them who glance through this book may feel that they have had very little mention. That is true and we apologize to them. They were not one of the deliberate omissions! It is rather that they would require another book to themselves. We are certainly not unmindful of the very important roles they play ranging from simply 'holding the fort' to helping to get priorities right. As onlookers they see much of the game and are, therefore, important members of the business – not to mention the family.

Computers

There has been limited mention of computers in what we have written and that might surprise some. The reason for that is not that we are not computer specialists ourselves but because what we have offered is specifically for the farm manager. We know of some who do have 'on farm' facilities, using them effectively for both planning and control purposes – especially, one suspects, the latter. They are however still in the minority, and a report published in 1984 by the Centre of Management in Agriculture indicates that only 6000 farmers (a mere 5% of all UK farms over 20 hectares) were using computers. Extensive use is, of course, made of such systems in the agricultural industry at large, from global purposes to bureau-based accountants or veterinary practices; but even so, again to quote the CMA survey, 'nine out of ten farmers do not use a computer as a farm business management aid'. Although the range of both hardware and software continues to be extended and costs are falling, it does appear that it will be some time before the computer will really 'invade' the farm. The situation may be different now, and different again in ten years time. A book published in 1986* indicates the scope for using microcomputers on the farm, including the important area of information storage and retrieval. But we still do not envisage rapid change.

The environment

There are few more topical and important subjects at the moment than the environment, and we are conscious that we have made little direct comment

---

*Moverley, J. (1986) *Microcomputers in Agriculture.* Collins Professional and Technical Books, London.

on this subject. We have, of course, indicated in our diagrammatic view of management that all management takes place within the context of a wider environment – the economic, political, social, legal and natural.

This view of the environment is not confined to the 'green' issues that are at the forefront of so much current discussion; we see those issues as merely one part (albeit an important part) of the much wider 'external environment' within which managers have to manage their own 'internal environment'. Seen in this way environmental issues have entered our text throughout, but any detailed discussion of such a wide ranging and influential set of issues would, as we explained at the outset, be well beyond the scope of this book.

CONCLUSIONS

Managers, not super-managers

First, a matter of perspective. Our book has been about management for managers, not for, or in order to try to create, super-managers. We do not envisage that anyone who reads it will want to rush away to embark on an orgy of objective-setting, planning, decision-making and control. What we hope is that some encouragement and some guidelines have been provided that will be of some assistance when those jobs have to be done, as surely they must be.

Profits

Now a last word about profits. It is a word and concept that has, not unnaturally, often appeared in this book. Yet we hope that 'profit' has not dominated the book – but rather taken its place alongside many other matters that are important. We should not wish this statement, moreover, to imply that a normally healthy attitude to the need to make profit is anything but very important. On occasions profit may take second place, but over time, it is profits which permit survival. None of the subject matter of this book is important for itself. Each subject is part of a means to an end. It is all part and parcel of effective management which will become reflected – within the talents and capabilities of all the individuals involved – in an ability to generate profits, to permit growth and to enable a business and its employment opportunities to continue. Profitability in this context must never be overlooked.

Judgement

If profit has been a well-used word in this book there is another that we believe could be running it a close race: it is the word 'judgement'. We have used it again and again. It is not easy to define; it is close to the word 'discretion'. It suggests an ability to weigh up any situation – the quantifiable and the non-quantifiable elements – and to reach a decision that at the very least proves not to be bad. It may well be that the ability of a manager to do just that is his most important quality; more important even than to achieve a particular profit level. It is very important, therefore, that self-employed managers should assume, and that salaried managers should be given, the authority that permits them fully to exercise their discretion and judgement. Managers, in short, must manage; they must be allowed to, and must train themselves to do it.

Getting it all right

Drucker says that what is wanted is 'the right strategy, not razzle-dazzle tactics'. We agree. But that should not imply that day-to-day decisions – which are often tactical in nature – are not important. The strategic and the tactical are important. It has been our observation that the best and most successful managers are, with the help of others, doing the right things and doing them well. The big things and the little things matter; getting it all right is a daunting task. It's called management.

Postscript

We have not quite finished; we wish to add a personal note.

Many books written by academics have their origins in lecture notes and teaching. For us the origins have been slightly different, coming instead from the countless conversations that we have had with farmers throughout this country and in many others. Sometimes these conversations have been face to face with individuals, but very often they have been with audiences at farmers' meetings. Between us we have been involved in hundreds of such meetings: with professional associations and with farming unions, at conferences and discussion groups, in colleges and church halls, in hotels, pubs and in farmhouses.

Throughout these experiences, we have been working in close proximity to each other at Reading University – one as an agricultural economist specializing in farm business management and the other originally 'doing the job' on the University's farms, but latterly as a teaching colleague. Over the years we have become aware that, despite our different backgrounds, we have often been thinking and saying the same kind of things. It was this common ground, stemming largely from evening speaking and from our work in the University, which led to our decision, ten years ago, to write a book. Since then we have continued to work together closely in the management of our University's Farm Management Unit.

When invited to write a second edition of *The Farmer as Manager* we had no desire to change either the title or the general style of the book. We still see it, not as a textbook covering the entire field of farm management, but rather as a collection of thoughts, based on some of the topics that we have discussed with farming audiences and taught to students up and down the country. If the reader has received any help at all from what he or she reads here, we will feel that we have been able to repay some of the benefits, friendship and hospitality that we have both been privileged to enjoy on these many occasions.

Index

In order to facilitate easy and helpful use, this index has been restricted deliberately to the *main* concepts and topics that have been discussed and page references have, in the main, been limited to those parts of the text where the items listed have been given their principal consideration or mention. No names of other authors have been included in this index, but any author whose work has been referred to in the text has also been included in the appropriate 'guide to selected further reading'. With one or two exceptions, the material contained in the final chapter, most of which summarizes what has preceded it, has also been excluded from the index.

acquiring resources 92–9, 106–7
advisers-consultants 89, 92, 95, 121, 134, 143, 189, 190–1
allocatable fixed costs 131–3
analysis of trading results 121–9
assets 141–2

balance sheets 141–4
  limitations of 144
  ratios 142–4
budgetary control 61–9
budgeting 60–1, 134–41
  break even 138
  cash flows 65, 139–40
  complete 134–6
  difficulties of 134
  need for different kinds 134
  partial 34, 49, 86, 113, 133, 136–8
buying 106–7
  example of 108–9

capital
  definitions 117–18
  in balance sheet 141–2
  return on 144–52
  types of 144–6
cash flows 65, 139–40
communications 164–5
comparative analysis 70, 126–9
complete budgets 134–6
computers 65, 67, 89, 140, 202
contractors 95

control 58–72
  essence of 60
  importance of 58–60
  inability to 68
  need for action 69–71
  physical nature of 60
  use of budgets in
    annual 63–5
    short period 65–8
co-operation 107–8, 189
costs, *see* inputs *and* fixed costs

decision-making 44–57, 112–14
  adequate time for 50–1
  components of 46–50
  examples of
    strategic decision 51–5
    tactical decision 55–6
delegation 178–9
diminishing returns 80, 91
diversification 90–2, 105, 113, 130, 133

economic efficiency 76–7
effective demand 76, 107
effectiveness 20, 193–4
efficiency measures 127
enterprise budgets-accounts 86, 129–33
environment 187–8, 202–3
equilibrium 77–9
excluded material 4–5, 198–9
exporting 187
external environment 11, 24

Farm Management Pocketbook 86
financial management 117–54
  accounts 121–33
  balance sheets 141–6
  budgets and cash flows 134–41
  diagrammatic view of 119–20
  financial planning, example 37–9
  investment appraisal 146–53
fixed costs 88–92, 129–33

gearing 143
gross margin(s) 82–92, 129–33, 137
  normalized gross margins 87
group trading 23, 106–8, 189

incentive payments 164
information for managers 183–92
  kinds of
    environmental 187–8
    financial 185–6
    intelligence 189
    international 186–7
    legal 186
    technical 184–5
  need for 183–4
  sources of 188–9
  storage and retrieval 189–90
input:output ratios 125–7
inputs 123–9
intended readership 3, 198–9
interest 152
internal environment 12
investment appraisal 146–53
  authors' checklist 151–2
  discounted yield 148–9
  intuitive approach 150–1
  net present value 148–9
  pay-back period 147–8
  return on outlay 147

job description 159–60
job satisfaction 155
judgement 34, 50–1, 80, 113, 141, 204

key results areas 21–2, 71, 194

labour management 95, 155–69
labour profiles 158–9
leadership 164–5
liabilities 141–4

linear programming 89
list of jobs 196
lower cost farming 130

management
  by crisis 32
  by objectives 20–2
  definition of 6–8
  diagrammatic view of 9–10
  literature 13–14
management accounting 122
management and investment
  income 126–7
managers
  individuality of 175–6
  influence of 173–4
  personal problems of 176–80
    boredom 176–7
    delegating 178–9
    insecurity 179–80
    isolation 176
    long, irregular hours 179
    organization of time 177–8
    recreational needs 179
    under-employment 177
  self appraisal of 23–4, 174–5
  their role 9–11, 99
managers' wives 202
marketing 102–16, 189
  farmers' role in 103–5, 114–15
  planning of, example 39–41
  relationship to production 102–3,
    107–8
market intelligence data 112–14, 189
marginal cost 79
marginal revenue 79
motivation 163–4

net margin 129–33
net worth 142–4

objectives 19–29
  advantages of 22–4
  determination of 20–2
  difficulties of 24–7
  long- and short-term 24
  management by 20–2
  need for 19–20
  personal 25–7
  quantifying 27–8
operating production plans 96–9

opportunity costs 113
ordered budgeting 89
output 123–9
overtrading 143

partial budgeting 34, 49, 86, 113, 133, 136–8
performance
 gap 70
 judgements about 126
 targets 60–1
 technical 12–13, 96–9
personal development 174–5
planning 31–43
 adjustments to 34
 examples of
  employment 41–2
  finance 37–9
  marketing 39–41
  production 36–7
 failure of 35
 nature of 32
 time spent 35
priorities 97–8, 193–7
 importance of 193–4
 nature of 194–5
 ordering of 195
 sticking with 195–6
profit 12–13, 121–3, 144–6, 203
 methods of improving 90–2
 sharing 164
profit and loss accounts 121–3
programme planning 87–8
production 75–101
 complexity of 75–6
 devising production plans 79–82, 87–90
  computerized methods 89
  subjective methods 80–1
 essential parts of 76
 operating the production plan 96–9
 relationship to market 102–3, 107–8

records 124–5
recruiting staff 158–61

redundancy 166
resources
 acquisition of 92–6, 106–7
 appraisal of 23
retirement of staff 165–6
return on capital 144–52
 existing 144–6
 fresh injections 146–7

selling 107–8
 example of 109–12
sensitivity analysis 138
single market (1992) 113
specialists 95, 121
spouses 202
square one questions 22
staff 155–69
 communications 164–5
 induction 161
 motivation and leadership 163–5
 payment 164
 planning 41–2, 156–8
 recruiting and interviewing 158–61
 reducing numbers 165–7
 supervision 99
 training 161–3
standard man days 157
standards of performance 126–9

taxation 120–1
technical efficiency 77, 86
theory of the firm 77–9
timeliness 95
trading accounts 121–3
 adjustments to 123–5
training 161–3
 management 162–3
 skills 161–2
 supervisory 162

unallocatable fixed costs 131–3
uncertainty and risk 35, 98–9, 138
utility 102–3, 107

variable costs, *see* gross margin